THE WORLD'S COMMERCIAL
AIRLINES

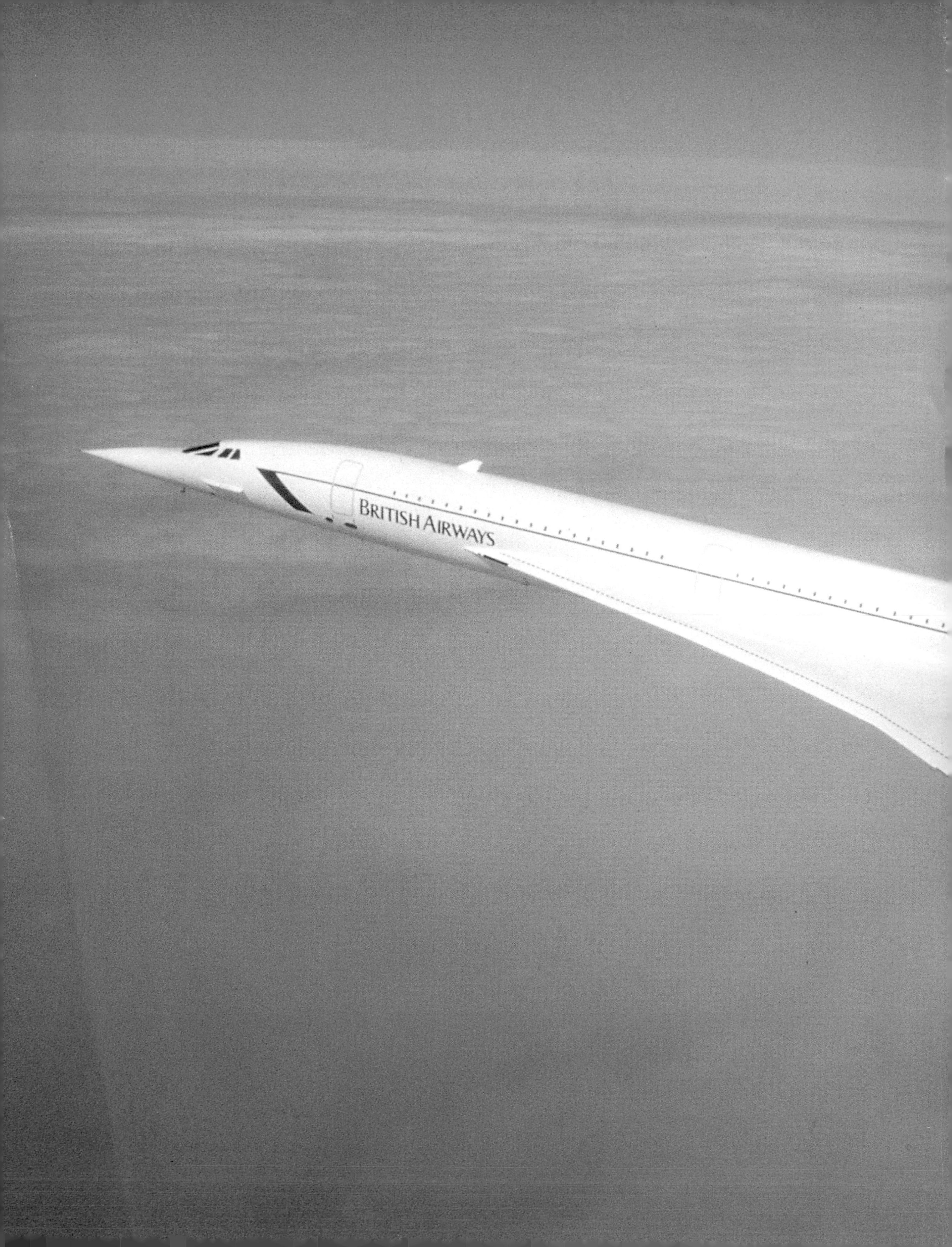
BRITISH AIRWAYS

THE WORLD'S COMMERCIAL
AIRLINES

Michael J.H. Taylor

Grange
BOOKS

PAGES 2-3
British Airways Concorde, one of seven such
supersonic aircraft on its books

THESE PAGES
airBaltic Avro International RJ70, received in
March 1996

Published in 1998 by
Grange Books
An imprint of Grange Books Plc
The Grange
Units 1-6 Kingsnorth Industrial Estate
Hoo. Nr Rochester, Kent
ME3 9ND

1 84013 000 8

Printed in China

Introduction

Many commercial airlines, like other businesses, traded through a roller-coaster existence during the 1980s and early 90s as recession squeezed profits. Some airlines which were household names even disappeared. Yet airports have announced successive years of major passenger growth.

Airliner manufacturing companies took casualties too, and Fokker of the Netherlands filed for bankruptcy in 1996, the 80 or so users of Fokker aircraft relying immediately thereafter on continuing support for nearly 1,200 aircraft from Fokker Services, a company of the new Fokker Aviation holdings that brought together Fokker businesses not affected by the bankruptcy.

Happily, not all is doom and gloom by a very long way and many believe that the world airline business has now finally beaten off recession. What evidence is there for this? Apart from an average 4.7 per cent increase in passenger volume at airports worldwide in the latest accounting year – with Europe, Asia and the Pacific Rim leading the march (expected to rise above 5 per cent) – several airline operators have demonstrated outstanding leaps in profitability. The movement of cargo, too, is predicted to rise at an even greater rate, with the present world freighter fleet of 1,200 or so aircraft expected to almost double by the year 2015.

Equally significant is the fact that the production of major airliners has recently been stepped up to meet growing demand. Between January and mid-August 1996, Airbus Industrie took 234 firm orders for its airliners, worth more than $16 billion. For the whole of 1996 Airbus Industrie expected to sell some 300 aircraft, three times the figure for 1995. For its part, Boeing has increased production rates on its 737, 747, 767 and 777, intending to produce 26.5 to 29 airliners of the entire current range (including 757s) per month in the first half of 1997, increasing to 36 by the third quarter of that year.

A major trend for airlines has been to enter into co-operation agreements to co-ordinate aspects of their businesses and reduce running costs, the intention being to share some non-core resources and thereby save money by avoiding too much duplication or spare capacity. A good example of this is Sabena World Airlines (*see* under Belgium). It has become common for airlines to form alliances to allow them to offer routes shared with other airlines, while some agreements between operators go further still and actually adopt crew-sharing on particular flights.

The World's Commercial Airlines has been written to provide an insight into airline operators from all regions. While the mainstays of the book are the scheduled passenger airlines flying dedicated airliners over established route networks plus important passenger/cargo charter operators, some smaller airlines are also included, where appropriate, to provide a balanced overview, especially if they represent the sole carrier of a nation or are particularly important for operating within sparsely populated regions. But not all the hundreds (if not thousands) of airlines can be included. To meet this challenge, representative companies have been targeted from all continents, particularly those that are IATA (International Air Transport Association) members, to offer a general survey of the current scene in the movement of passengers and freight.

Great effort has been made to ensure accuracy, but the information provided should be taken only as a general guide; the publisher and author accept no liability for any errors or inaccuracies that may have occurred, including those caused by the passage of time. Data has been based on information received in mid-1996 and references to the 'latest' figures refer to the last full operating year up to that time or the latest figures then available, unless stated otherwise.

The author would like to offer special thanks to IATA, Mrs Aruna Singh for her kind assistance in obtaining material on airlines operating in India, Peter Middleton, and the huge number of airlines that responded to requests for material.
MJHT 1996

To avoid the need to repeat aircraft manufacturers' names throughout the text, the following principal companies produce (or have produced) the following airliners

Airbus Industrie (France/Spain/Germany/UK): A300, A310, A319, A320, A321, A330, A340
Airtech (Indonesia/Spain): CN 235
Antonov (Ukraine): An-2, An-12, An-24, An-26, An-32, An-72, An-124, An-225
Avions de Transport Régional (France/Italy): ATR 42, ATR 72
Avro International (UK): RJ70, RJ85, RJ100, RJ115
Beriev (Russia): Be 32
Boeing (USA): 707, 727, 737, 747, 757, 767, 777
Bombardier Canadair (Canada): Challenger, Global Express, Regional Jet
Bombardier de Havilland (Canada): Dash 8
British Aerospace (BAe) (UK): BAe 146
British Aerospace and Aérospatiale (UK/France): Concorde
CASA (Spain): C-212 Aviocar
Daimler-Benz Aerospace (Germany): Dornier 228, 328
de Havilland Canada (now Bombardier de Havilland)(Canada): DHC-5 Buffalo, DHC-6 Twin Otter, Dash 7
EMBRAER (Brazil): EMB-110 Bandeirante, EMB-120 Brasilia, EMB-145, Xingu
Fokker (Netherlands): 50, 70, 100, 130, F27 Friendship, F28 Fellowship
Harbin (China): Y-12
IAI (Israel): Arava
Ilyushin (Russia): Il-18, Il-62, Il-76, Il-86, Il-96, Il-114
IPTN (Indonesia): N-250
Jetstream Aircraft (UK): Jetstream 31, Super 31, 41, ATP
Let (Czech Republic): L 410, L 420, L 610
Lockheed Martin (USA): L-100 Hercules (or Commercial Hercules), TriStar
McDonnell Douglas (USA): DC-8, DC-9, DC-10, MD-11, MD-80 series, MD-81, MD-82, MD-83, MD-87, MD-88
Pilatus Britten-Norman (UK): Islander, Trislander
PZL-Mielec (Poland): An-2 (*see also* Antonov)
Raytheon (USA): Beech 1900
Saab (Sweden): 340, 2000
Shaanxi (China): Y8
Shorts (UK): 330, 360
Sud-Est/Aérospatiale (France): Caravelle
Tupolev (Russia): Tu-134, Tu-154, Tu-204
Xi'an (China): Y7
Yakovlev (Russia): Yak-40, Yak-42

*The term **revenue passenger-kilometres** has been abbreviated to **RPK**, **available passenger-kilometres** to **APK** and **available seat-kilometre** to **ASK***

OPPOSITE
New Boeing airliners awaiting delivery to customers in Singapore, the USA and Germany

BELOW
Malev Fokker 70, part of the privatized airline's modernized fleet

Afghanistan

Ariana Afghan Airlines is the only airline currently operating into Afghanistan and has Bagram as its base, an airport approximately one hour by road from Kabul. Its genealogy can be traced back to January 1955, when an enterprising American transferred several war-surplus Douglas C-47 Dakotas from India, where they had been operating on a casual basis. The move established an air service in Afghanistan where none existed, soon to be formalized by the Afghan Government as Aryana Afghan Airlines. In 1957 an agreement was reached between the Royal Afghan Government and the United States International Co-operation Administration to formally finance the airline, leading to incorporation as a limited company, with 51 per cent of shares held by the Government and 49 per cent by Pan American World Airways. The present name was then adopted.

Concurrent with changes to the airline came development of the nation's air facilities, with assistance from the US Federal Aeronautics Administration. Other assistance from the USSR led to the development of an airport and terminal at Kabul, and it was to Kabul that Ariana moved its operational headquarters in 1965. The airline's first jet transport, a Boeing 727, was acquired in 1968. Over the years foreign assistance in operating the airline and training personnel was gradually reduced, and by the early 1970s on-the-job training by Pan American technicians to improve the airline's technical abilities was nearing an end, leaving Ariana in a strong position to continue on its own merit.

Ariana has a mixed fleet of five 727s, two An-24s, An-26s, two Yak-40s and a single Tu-154M, with which it currently carries a yearly total of 40,000-45,000 passengers. International services are to and from Delhi, Amritsar, Dubai, Tashkent and Moscow, Jeddah, Frankfurt and Paris, accumulating approximately 66.29 million revenue passenger-kilometres (RPK).

Ariana Afghan Airlines
Address: Post Office Box 76, Kabul, Afghanistan.
Telephone: +93 21015/16/17

Bakhtar Afghan Airlines offers scheduled and charter domestic services, flying from Kabul to Kandahar, Bamiyan, Chaghcharan, Herat, Faizabad, Kunduz, Mazare Sharif and Maimana. Its fleet includes the Yak-40.

Albania

This nation's fledgling airline is ADA Air, founded in February 1992, in which year it carried 6,339 passengers and accumulated 1.7 million RPK. Its current equipment comprises one EMB-110P2 Bandeirante and one Yak-40, with which it operates scheduled daily services between Tirana and Bari and thrice-weekly between Tirana and Athens. The number of passengers carried yearly has risen to 13,035, with RPK standing at 3.5 million.

ADA Air
Address: Rr Reshit Collaku, P.5, Tirana, Albania.
Telephone: +355 42 248 08 or 230 89
Fax: +355 42 325 89

Algeria

Algeria has an active air transport system, including 28 airports nationwide. Recent figures suggest that well over 3 billion RPK are now flown yearly by Air Algérie (the flag carrier), and substantially over 20 million tonne-kilometres of cargo.

Air Algérie began as Compagnie Générale de Transports Aériens, in 1946. In 1953 it absorbed Compagnie Air Transport, by which time it was operating regular services. Air Algérie was nationalized in 1972.

Apart from a large network of scheduled international services to destinations in Africa, the Middle East and Europe, Air Algérie conducts scheduled domestic flights, cargo operations (principally with three Hercules freighters), other charter work and agricultural services. Headquartered at Algiers, its passenger aircraft fleet comprises 31 pure jet airliners, including no fewer than 15 737-200s and 11 727-200s. Very modern large capacity airliners are represented by three 767-300s and two A310s, while seven turboprop F27s are the smallest aircraft of the main fleet.

Angola

Linhas Aéreas de Angola, better known simply as TAAG Angola Airlines, is one of over 200 IATA members and is nationalized. Founded in 1939 as Divisão de Exploracão dos Transportes Aéreos de Angola (DTA) by the Portuguese Government (Ministry of Colonies), it operated only comparatively small-size aircraft over domestic and regional routes for many years and it was not until 1973 that its present name was adopted.

Angola has 17 airports handling scheduled

flights, and TAAG as the principal airline has Luanda on the east coast as its base from which to offer a network of domestic services and international flights within Africa and to destinations in Europe and the Americas. In addition, TAAG provides charter flights through two subsidiary companies, one of which is Angola Air Charter which has four Hercules cargo freighters and a similar number of Boeing 707-320Cs.

The main TAAG fleet relies heavily on Boeing airliners, including one 707-320B and five more modern 737-200s. A TriStar, plus two Il-62Ms and two Yak-40s from Russia, comprise the remainder of the pure-jet fleet, supported by six F27 turboprop airliners. Passenger-kilometres total is believed to be about 1.2 billion.

Also operating out of Luanda is Air Nacoia, a fairly new airline founded in 1993 and flying a single 727-200.

Antigua and Barbuda

Antigua and Barbuda in the West Indies have two airports offering scheduled flights. The two main airlines based on the tiny island of Antigua are naturally occupied in providing services to the many Leeward and Windward islands, from Anguilla in the north to Grenada in the south, with other destinations as far south as Trinidad and Tobago. The main airline is Liat, offering scheduled and charter flights using nine Dash 8 and six Twin Otter turboprop airliners. After 21 years of ownership by a coalition of regional governments, Liat passed into the private sector in 1995.

Seagreen Air Transport, also operating from V C Bird International Airport at Antigua's capital of Saint John's in the north of the island, has a single cargo-carrying 707 which is occupied on charter flights. (*See also* BWIA under Trinidad and Tobago.)

Argentina

Argentina has 42 airports handling scheduled flights and a passenger-kilometres total of more than 9 billion. Of its airlines, Aérolineas Argentinas and Austral Líneas Aéreas are the principal carriers and both are members of IATA.

Aérolineas Argentinas was formed in May 1949, when all the existing airlines in the country merged into a state organization, with the exception of the military-run LADE. It thereafter became the nation's flag airline, though at the present time 83.35 per cent of its shares are owned by Iberia of Spain, a situation that is soon likely to change. Most scheduled flights are to destinations in the Americas, while others take in New Zealand and several European cities including London, Madrid, Frankfurt, Zurich and Rome. Its fleet has a substantial Boeing representation, with six 747s, 11 737s and seven 727s, joined by three A310s, six MD-88s and three F28s.

Aérolineas Argentinas
Address: Bouchard 547-8 Piso,
Buenos Aires, Argentina.
Telephone: +54 1 317 3269
Fax: +54 1 317 3585

Austral Líneas Aéreas was founded in 1971 and has established a substantial domestic network of services. Its 16 aircraft range from two CN 235 turboprop airliners to seven DC-9s, five newer MD-81/83s and two BAC One-Elevens.

Of other Argentine passenger airlines, only

Líneas Aéreas Privadas Argentinas has a fleet encompassing large aircraft, operating scheduled and charter international and domestic flights with a single 757, six or seven 737s and two Saab 340s. Interestingly, Aries Del Sur flies cargo operations with leased large-capacity jets.

Armenia

Armenian Airlines was established in 1993, having been formed as an offshoot of Aeroflot following the break-up of the former USSR. Armenia has two main airports and a particularly busy air transport system that is thought to accumulate 5.5 billion RPK and nearly 50 million cargo tonne-kilometres per year. Its all-Russian fleet comprises nine Tu-134s, ten Tu-154Bs, two Il-86s and a Yak-40, while the expected future purchase of two European Airbus A310s had not materialized into firm orders by September 1996.

Armenian Airlines
Address: Airport Zvartnots, 375042 Yerevan-42, Republic of Armenia.

Aruba

A small island of the Lesser Antilles, Dutch Caribbean, Aruba has its own airline, known as Air Aruba, which began operations in 1988 and has since expanded its network considerably. It undertakes domestic services to two destinations, presumably using its EMB-120 Brasilia, and flies international routes with a DC-9 and three MD-80s, the latter to nearby Caracas in Venezuela and various points in the USA, with some co-operation from USAir.

Australia

With a land mass of almost 3 million sq miles (7,682,000 sq km) but a population of only 18 million, it is hardly surprising that in Australia a large number of airlines operate scheduled services to and from well over 400 domestic airports.

In addition to the domestic routes offered by the two largest airlines (*see* Ansett Australia and Qantas) that also have important international destinations, there are many other smaller airlines undertaking only or principally scheduled and/or charter domestic flights. Some are run by or affiliated to Ansett and Qantas (*see* later paragraphs). A good example is National Jet Systems in South Australia, a very important airline with a large fleet of pure-jet (including BAe 146/Avro International RJ70s) and turboprop airliners to ply the Australian Airlink connections for Qantas and undertake other work.

Before detailing the principal international airlines of Australia, it is worth taking a closer look at one or two more smaller regional operators, as these are vital to the infrastructure of a nation with only six persons per sq mile average population density (compared with over 620 per sq mile for the UK).

Hazelton Airlines is one of the largest regional airlines in Australia, providing air services to 21 destinations in the eastern states. It was founded in 1953 as a charter operator with a single-engined aircraft, expanding to become a major aerial agricultural and charter company and, in 1975, commenced airline operations. The business was owned by the Hazelton family until 1993, when Hazelton Airlines acquired all shares in Hazelton Air Services, becoming a listed public company on the Australian Stock Exchange that December.

During 1995, Hazelton acquired a further five aircraft, its total fleet now comprising six Saab 340Bs, four Fairchild Metro 23s, three Piper Navajo Chieftains and two Cessna 310s; its two Shorts 360s were withdrawn in June/July 1995. In 1995-96 Hazelton transported nearly 400,000 passengers. It

has about 272 full-time employees at seven locations.

Hazelton Airlines
Address: PO Box 12, Cudal, NSW 2864, Australia.
Telephone: +61 63 61 5815
Fax: +61 63 64 2294

Celebrating 30 years in business (in 1997), Kendell Airlines is today the largest of Australia's regional airlines, achieving a 60 per cent growth during 1995-96 through the addition of services from Sydney to Canberra (part of the Capital Shuttle service with Ansett Australia, offering 22 flights daily), Albury, Wagga Wagga and, from the summer of 1996, Coffs Harbor and Ballina. Further expansion in NSW is planned, in association with Ansett Australia, Kendell's major affiliate. In total, Kendell serves a network of 20 centres in four states and the Northern Territory from Melborne, Adelaide and Sydney.

ABOVE
Aérolineas Argentinas Airbus A310

OPPOSITE
Air Algérie Airbus A310

To cope with increased services, Kendell took in two more Saab 340s in 1996, providing a total fleet of 11 Saab 340s and seven Metro 23s. In a full year, about 750,000 passengers are carried. Some 350 staff are employed.

Kendell Airlines (Australia)
Address: 86 Baylis Street, Wagga Wagga,
NSW 2650, Australia.
Telephone: +61 69 220 100
Fax: +61 69 220 116

Ansett Australia, as one of Australia's two big airlines, operates domestic, regional and international services with an expanding fleet of modern aircraft. Its countrywide network of domestic destinations is operated from the hubs of Adelaide, Alice Springs, Brisbane, Canberra, Darwin, Gold Coast, Hobart, Launceston (Tasmania), Melbourne, Perth and Sydney, and includes the services of co-operating partner airlines such as Aeropelican, Air Facilities, Airnorth, August Airways, Flight West Airlines, Hazelton, Impulse, Kendell, Sabair, Skywest, Tamair and Yanda Airlines. Regional routes encompass those to Norfolk Island, Christmas and Cocos Islands, and Whitsunday Islands.

Ansett Australia's international operations began in 1993, following the Australian Government's 'One

TOP
Kendell Airlines Saab 340 with the new tail design
ABOVE
National Jet Systems Avro International RJ70

RIGHT
Ansett Australia Boeing 747-300 'Spaceship' (rear) and Airbus A320

Nation' statement of 26 February 1992 in which other Australian airlines (in addition to Qantas) were to be allowed to fly internationally, while Qantas would be permitted domestic routes. Ansett Australia today flies to and from the hubs of Denpasar and Jakarta in Indonesia, Kuala Lumpur in Malaysia, Hong Kong, T'aipei in Taiwan, and Osaka in Japan, while commercial alliances with many other international airlines (that include United Airlines, Singapore Airlines, Cathay Pacific, Malaysia Airlines, All Nippon Airways, Swissair, Austrian, Aérolineas Argentinas, Garuda, Virgin Atlantic and South African Airways) has allowed Ansett to offer a near worldwide Frequent Flyer network in association with the flights of these partners. Recent developments have included arrangements with Air China, China Eastern and China Southern for Ansett passengers to travel on to major Chinese cities.

The Ansett Australia fleet comprises three 747-300s, nine 767-200/300ERs, 22 737-300s, five 727LRs, a 727 freighter, 15 A320-200s, 12 BAe 146-200/300s plus two 146 freighters, and four F28-4000s. Four more A320s will be delivered in 1997 which, along with three additional 767s and a 737 to

be delivered this financial year, will not only increase overall fleet capacity by 10 per cent but allow the 727s and F28s to be retired.

Currently employing over 16,000 people in more than 20 countries, Ansett Australia carried 12,420,000 passengers in the latest accounting year, and recorded an RPK total of 12,342 million. It has an interesting history, starting in 1935 when Myles Ansett first registered Ansett Airways, acquired a Porterfield aircraft and recruited a pilot, having been unable to continue his small road taxi service. Flights began on 17 February 1936 and in 1937 the airline was incorporated as a public company. The present name was adopted on 4 October 1990 from the former Ansett Airlines of Australia.

Ansett Australia
Address: 13/501 Swanston Street, Melbourne, Victoria 3000, Australia.
Telephone: +61 3 623 1211
Fax: +61 3 623 1114

Qantas Airways is thought to be the world's 11th largest airline and the second largest in the Asia-

Pacific region in terms of RPK. As the nation's flag airline, it has Australia's largest fleet of aircraft, with a core of 93 jets used on international and main domestic routes. The core fleet comprises 18 747-400 *Longreach*, six 747-300s with extended upper decks, five 747-200Bs, two 747SPs, 15 767-300ERs, seven 767-200ERs, 20 737-400s, 16 737-300s and four A300B4s. A further two 737-400s and two 767-300ERs were to be received during 1996, and options on 22 possible new aircraft for the future include 16 747-400s.

In addition, regional carriers in the Qantas Group (Eastern Australia Airlines, Southern Australia Airlines, Sunstate Airlines and Airlink) operate 46 aircraft, comprising nine BAe 146s, 14 Dash 8s, three Jetstream 31s and a Jetstream 32, five Twin Otters, six Shorts 360s, two Cessna 404 Titans and six Titan Air Ambulances, making a total Qantas Group fleet of 139 aircraft.

The latest figures available at the time of writing indicate that the Qantas core airline carried 14.42 million passengers over international and domestic routes during a 12-month period and, with regional carriers added, the group total became 16.05 million.

The Group has the largest share of the domestic market in terms of RPK, at 51.2 per cent, while Qantas recorded a 40.3 per cent share of the total passenger market into and out of Australia when excluding Australia Asia Airlines' services to T'aipei in Taiwan. Interestingly, Australia Asia Airlines itself is a subsidiary of Qantas, operating a 767-300ER and leasing the two 747SPs from its parent company.

The Qantas scheduled route network takes in 94 destinations in 27 countries, when including the Solomon Islands, Vanuatu, Chicago, New York, San Francisco, Toronto, Vancouver, Honiara, Mount Hagen and Port Vila that are code-share services operated by other airlines on behalf of Qantas. As part of the offered overall Qantas network, British Airways also connects London to many cities in various continents served by Qantas, including eight in North America, while a subsidiary of British Airways, British Asia Airlines, adds the Hong Kong to T'aipei route. The bulk of Qantas destinations are in Australia (52) and the Asia/Pacific region (25), while New Zealand accounts for three, the UK one, Italy one, Germany one, USA seven, Canada two, South Africa one and Zimbabwe one.

Qantas was registered as Queensland and Northern Territory Aerial Services Limited on 16 November 1920. It began by offering joyrides and air taxi work, adding regular scheduled airmail and passenger services on 2 November 1922 when the inaugural service carried Australia's first official airmail from Charleville to Cloncurry, a distance of 573 miles (923 km) that took two days.

In 1934 Qantas Empire Airways Limited was formed, with Britain's Imperial Airways (forerunner of British Airways) holding half the shares and beginning a partnership that served both airlines well. In 1947, the Australian Government purchased all shares in Qantas but in 1991 it decided to privatize the airline and offered 49 per cent for sale. British Airways repurchased a 25 per cent stake. Qantas shares were first listed on the Australian Stock Exchange in July 1995. Today, the airline employs some 29,500 people.

Qantas Airways
Address: Qantas Centre, Building A/7, 203 Coward Street, Mascot 2020, Australia.
Telephone: +61 2 691 3472
Fax: +61 2 691 4187

Qantas Airways Boeing 747s in special Aboriginal colours. The more typical tail livery remains unaltered

Austria

Austria has six airports handling scheduled services and a similar number of principal airlines. Eurosky Airlines, a member of IATA, is based in Vienna and operates eight Fairchild Metro 23s as a regional carrier, while Rheintalflug at Bregenz has four Dash 8s with which to fly scheduled domestic and regional routes, some in alliance with Austrian Airlines, plus charter work.

An important player is Lauda Air Luftfahrt, founded by the Formula One racing driver of that name, which began charter and air taxi services in a modest way in 1985. Two years later scheduled services were added, followed by its first scheduled international operations in 1990. Expansion has been rapid and in 1996 its fleet of 17 jets include five 767s-300ERs, six Regional Jets and four 737s, while orders will subsequently place four 777s and two 737-800s into its livery.

Austrian Air Transport is a small international passenger and cargo charter concern with the majority of its shares held by Austrian Airlines, which supplies its aircraft. Larger is Tyrolean Airways, whose fleet of more than 30 aircraft includes 17 Dash 8s and seven earlier Dash 7 turboprop transports plus several Fokker 70 twin-jets. Again, Austrian Airlines is a shareholder, and scheduled and charter flights are made to many points in Europe.

After the Second World War, the Allies did not permit civil aviation activities in Austria until the State Treaty was signed in 1955. On 30 September 1957, Austrian Airlines was founded, commencing flight operations on 31 March 1958 with four chartered Vickers Viscounts. Its first pure-jet airliner, a Caravelle VI-R, was put into use in February 1963, and in April 1969 the airline inaugurated a transatlantic service (Vienna-Brussels-New York) in co-operation with Sabena using a chartered Boeing 707. Today, as the principal airline of Austria, it employs 3,873 persons and has a fleet of 31 airliners, comprising two A340-200s, four A310-300s, three A321s, seven MD-81s, six MD-82s, two MD-83s and five MD-87s, plus two Fokker 70s. Seven A320s, five A321s and two Fokker 70s were then on order.

Austrian Airlines has an international and domestic network that covers 83 cities in 48 countries on four continents, totalling 155,000 unduplicated route-kilometres. Charter flights are also offered to 80 destinations, including holiday resorts in the Caribbean, the Mediterranean, the Canary Islands, Kenya, India and the Maldives.

Austrian Airlines (Österreichische Luftverkehrs AG)
Address: Fontanastrasse 1, A-1107 Vienna, Austria.
Telephone: +43 1 1766-0
Fax: +43 1 68 55 05

Azerbaijan

With only one airport offering scheduled flights, the republic has Azerbaijan Hava Yollari as its flag-carrying airline. The total passenger-kilometres flown is unclear since the airline was established in 1992, but in 1990, prior to its formation, the state reportedly recorded a figure of nearly 5 billion passenger-kilometres for its total air activities. Offering a full range of international, domestic and charter services, it has a fleet of nine An-26s and An-32s, 15 Tu-154Bs and Ms, eight or nine Tu-134s and 14 Yak-40s, plus two 727-200s and one or two 707-320Cs as the only Western types.

Bahamas

There are three main airlines based on the island group, all small in fleet size. Laker Airways Bahamas is an international/regional and domestic scheduled airline founded in 1992 by Briton, Sir Freddie Laker. With its headquarters in Florida but operating out of Freeport in the Bahamas, it flies two 727-200s mainly on a network to the USA and is the only airline of the three to be a member of IATA.

Bahamasair was founded in 1973 and the sole shareholder is the Government. It, too, offers international/regional and domestic flights, though its destinations to the USA are fewer than those undertaken by Laker. Using both Freeport and Nassau as operating bases, it has a fleet of five Dash 8 turboprop airliners and two 737 twin-jets.

The third of the airlines is Taino Airways, which undertakes scheduled regional and domestic services, plus emergency ambulance work, with a single Shorts 330 and an EMB-110 Bandeirante.

Bashkortostan

This republic of the Russian Federation has an area of some 55,400 sq miles (143,500 sq km) and a population of a little over 4 million. It has one principal airline flying scheduled/charter domestic and regional services, known as Sterlitamak Airlines. Operating out of Sterlitamak, some 80 miles

(130 km) south of the capital Ufa, its fleet comprises An-2 biplanes and An-24 twin-props.

Bahrain

Gulf Air is a member of IATA and the flag-carrying airline of four nations, operating a modern fleet over international and regional networks. Its international services stretch from New York and Houston in the USA to Sydney in Australia, taking in many destinations in Asia, the Middle East, Africa and several European capital and major cities.

Founded in 1950, it is owned and jointly administered by the governments of Bahrain, Oman, Qatar and the United Arab Emirates and thereby has its hub bases in four separate locations, at Muscat

(Masqat) in Oman and Doha (Ad-Dawhah) in Qatar as well as in Abu Dhabi and Bahrain, the latter having only a single airport handling scheduled flights at the capital of Manama. Its fleet comprises 14 A320s and three A340s (of five delivered, with one more on order), 18 767-300s and one 757-200F Freighter, and perhaps five TriStars, while six A330s are on order. A subsidiary of the airline is Gulf Helicopters (*see* Qatar).

Gulf Air G.S.C.
Address: PO Box 138, Bahrain.
Telephone: +973 338 088
Fax: +973 323 021

ABOVE
Gulf Air Boeing 767-300

LEFT
Austrian Airlines Airbus A321 in Millennium livery, celebrating 1,000 years of Austria (996-1996), with portraits of famous people past and present, including Mozart, Strauss and Haydn

OPPOSITE TOP
Tyrolean Airways Fokker 70

Bangladesh

This nation has eight airports handling scheduled flights. Its national airline, Biman Bangladesh Airlines, was founded in 1972 and is a member of IATA operating out of Dhaka. Large capacity is handled by a fleet of five DC-10-30s and two A310-300s (the latter received in June and August 1996). Smaller airliners are two F28-4000s and two BAe ATPs. In addition to domestic and charter flights, its extensive international network takes in destinations as far apart as London, New York and Hong Kong.

Biman Bangladesh Airlines
Address: Biman Bhavan Motijheel,
1000 Dhaka, Bangladesh.
Telephone: +880 2 240 151
Fax: +880 2 863 005

Barbados

Grantley Adams International at the island's capital of Bridgetown is the only airport on Barbados handling scheduled flights. Carib Express became an indigenous airline using three BAe 146-100s supplied via BAe's AMO. However, according to BAe, the airline ceased operations in spring 1996. (*See also* BWIA under Trinidad and Tobago.)

Belarus

This republic, formerly a state of the USSR, has only one airport for scheduled flights at its capital Minsk. The national airline is Belarussian Airlines (or Belavia Byelorussian Association of Civil Aviation), founded in 1993 and offering an expanding network of scheduled services that cover destinations in Austria, Germany, Ireland, Israel, Poland and

Switzerland, while it also undertakes charter flights to points as far apart as China, India and Turkey, among others. As a splinter of Aeroflot, it has an all- Russian and Ukrainian fleet, comprising 25 An-24/26s, 19 Tu-134s, at least 14 Tu-154Bs, four Tu-154Ms, eight Yak-40s and an Il-86.

Belarussian Airlines (Belavia Byelorussian)
Address: Str 4, Minsk 220065, Belarus.
Telephone: +375 172 25 08 36
Fax: +375 172 25 15 66

Other Belarus airlines include Belair with two Il-76TDs for cargo and two Tu-134s and a Yak-40 for passenger charters, and Transaviaexport that is a major international cargo charter operator with 16 Il-76MDs.

Belgium

In addition to five airlines operating scheduled services, Belgium supports a wealth of charter companies flying large jets, plus a number with smaller aircraft for international air taxi and cargo work.

Airlines with large aircraft for charter operations include Air Belgium which is headquartered at Zaventem and flies a 757-200 and 737-400 on international inclusive tour and other work; ChallengAir at Brussels with leased DC-10s; Skyjet at Brussels with DC-10-30 and 737 jets; and Sobelair which is a Sabena subsidiary operating from Brussels with one leased 767-300 and six 737-200/300/400s (two -400s leased) for passenger and cargo charters to 13 countries in Europe, the Middle East and North Africa.

European Air Transport (EAT) based at Brussels National Airport in Zaventem has been owned by

DHL Worldwide Express since 1986 as its primary airline to transport urgent shipments across Europe. It is a member of IATA. Founded in 1971, its fleet comprises (as of 17 June 1996) three Fairchild Metros (FA4s) currently leased to Swift Air, nine Convair CV580s (three leased to Swift Air), six 727-100s and six 727-200s. EAT aircraft are engaged on DHL sectors at night, while day-time *ad hoc* charters are arranged on request using the CV580s and 727s. No passengers are carried, as reflected in the latest figure of 232,999 available ton-kilometres.

EAT employs 325 persons, of which 161 are pilots and 116 technicians. It also acts as a consultant for DHL in Europe on aviation matters, and in this secondary role subcontracts some 35 aircraft provided by 15 different carriers.

European Air Transport
Address: Hangar 4-5, B-1930 Zaventem, Belgium.
Telephone: +32 2 718 14 14
Fax: +32 2 718 15 55

Sabena Belgian World Airlines was founded in 1923 (under its full name Société Anonyme Belge pour l'Éxploitation de la Navigation Aérienne) out of the former SNETA. It is today the principal airline of Belgium and carried 5,000,951 passengers in the latest full year, achieving an RPK total of 8,620 million, and a load factor of 63 per cent when calculated against an APK total of 13,685 million. Some 9,486 persons were then employed.

The core fleet comprises four operational-leased A340-200/-300s (temporarily subleased to Air France, though the two A340-300s were to be reintegrated into the fleet in 1996), four A310-200/ -300s, three 747-200/-300s (the -200 leased) and 28 737s (including three financial-leased 737-400s and

OPPOSITE
Biman Bangladesh Airlines Airbus A310-300

TOP
European Air Transport Boeing 727s engaged
on DHL deliveries, with a Sobelair jet to the rear

ABOVE
One of two operational-leased McDonnell
Douglas DC-10-30CF convertible freighters
used by Sabena

six 737-500s, and 13 operational-leased 737-200s), plus two operational-leased DC-10-30CF convertible freighters for passengers or cargo.

The airline's extensive route network of 88 destinations in 46 countries includes a hub and spoke European system serving 60 destinations, plus services to the Middle East and Africa, Tokyo in Japan, Bangkok in Thailand, and some points in North America. Among the latest routes to be introduced is a new Macao service under a codeshare agreement with TAP Air Portugal, beginning 31 March 1996.

Shares in Sabena are now owned by Belgian investors and the Government (50.5 per cent) and Swissair (49.5 per cent), the collaboration with Swissair allowing close co-operation in areas such as sales, engineering and maintenance, information services, and passenger/cargo services.

Sabena Belgian World Airlines
Address: Sabena House 38, Brussels National Airport, B-1930 Zaventem, Belgium; or N.V. Sabena S.A., Avenue E. Mounieriaan 2, B-1200 Brussels, Belgium.
Telephone: +32 2 723 84 00
Fax: +32 2 723 83 99

Delta Air Transport, founded in 1966 and headquartered at Antwerp, is majority owned by Sabena. It undertakes scheduled passenger services to some 27 European destinations in Austria, France, Germany, Italy, Luxembourg, the Netherlands, Portugal, Spain, Switzerland and the UK using a mixed fleet of twin-jet, four-jet and twin-turboprop airliners. Having ordered no fewer than 23 Avro International RJ85s, this type of four-jet airliner will eventually replace existing BAe 146s and F28s; RJ85 deliveries began on 6 December 1995 (four received that month, eight for delivery in 1996, four in 1997, six in 1998 and one in 1999). At the time of writing, the received RJ85s complemented the eight existing BAe 146-200s (including four leased) and eight F28-1000/-3000/-4000s (all leased, including two leased from Sabena Leasing). The turboprop airliner fleet comprises ten EMB-120 Brasilias (one operated for KLM).

EuroBelgian Airlines, headquartered in Melsbroek, began operations in 1992 and offers both scheduled and charter flights from Brussels with a fleet of 12 Boeing 737-300/-400s. Six new aircraft ordered in 1995-96 are 737-300/-400/-800s.

VLM, or more fully Vlaamse Luchttransportmaatschappij, has been flying Fokker 50s since it started operations in 1993, taking its fourth aircraft on 15 March 1996 (with a fifth then still to be delivered). The airline links Antwerp, Düsseldorf/Mönchengladbach and Rotterdam with London City Airport.

Belize

This small Central American country, with a population of only 216,000, has nine airports handling scheduled flights. The main airport is Belize International, from which approximately 122,000 passenger departures are made yearly.

Indigenous airlines are small and serve the region, including Maya Airways with five Islanders and Tropical Air Services with two Twin Otters plus six Cessnas.

Bhutan

Bhutan is situated to the north of Bangladesh and has a population of over 816,000. It has one airport from which scheduled flights are made and its own

national airline, Druk Air, or Royal Bhutan Airlines. Founded in 1981, it operates two BAe 146-100s on scheduled services to points in Nepal, India and Thailand, plus charters.

Bolivia

This South American nation has 21 airports handling scheduled flights. The principal airline is Lloyd Aéreo Boliviano, which is mainly owned by the Government and VASP Brazilian Airlines. It is thought that its RPK total is considerably over 1,170 million. LAB has a fleet of one A310, six 727-100/200s, a single 707-320C and two F27s with which to operate domestic flights and those to some 17 destinations outside of its borders.

Bosnia and Herzegovina

Air Bosnia was founded in 1994 but had not yet begun flying at the time of writing.

Botswana

Founded in 1972, Air Botswana is the national airline, operating out of Gabarone, one of four airports handling scheduled flights. It is thought to have an RPK total of about 84 million and a cargo tonne-kilometre total of about 650,000, though these figures may be outdated. Its fleet comprises two ATR 42-320s and a BAe 146-100, used on domestic services and internationally to destinations in Kenya, Namibia, South Africa, Zambia and Zimbabwe.

Brazil

Brazil has a huge land mass of some 3.3 million square miles (8.5 million sq km) and a population of about 156 million. It is hardly surprising, therefore, that there are 139 airports handling scheduled flights and a considerable number of airlines offering extensive route networks.

Transbrasil, Varig and VASP, Brazil's main airlines, are all members of IATA. Transbrasil Airlines (Transbrasil Linhas Aéreas) was founded in 1955 and has an all-Boeing fleet of 11 767s, 12 737s and two 707-320Cs with which to operate to 20 domestic destinations, plus Argentina, the USA,

Austria and the Netherlands.

Varig (Viação Aérea Rio-Grandense) is the country's principal airline, flying from its main hub at Rio de Janeiro to 35 domestic and 31 foreign destinations. In the latest full year it carried 9,334,720 passengers. It has 19,000 employees, which include 5,011 aircrew. Subsidiaries are the domestic airlines Rio-Sul Serviços Aéreos Regionais S/A (flying seven 737-500s, ten EMB-120 Brasilias and nine Fokker 50s belonging to Varig) and Nordeste Linhas Aéreas (with nine EMB-110 Bandeirantes, four Brasilias and two Fokker 50s).

Varig was founded on 7 May 1927 as the first airline in Brazil and among the first in the world, its founder (Otto Ernst Meyer) having already organized survey and publicity flights with a Dornier Wal flying-boat. International services were inaugurated on 5 August 1942, connecting Pôrto Alegre to Montevideo using a de Havilland Dragon Rapide biplane. The airline's first jets were French Caravelles purchased in 1959. Today's fleet comprises four 767-300ERs, six 767-200ERs, five 747-300s, 25 737-300s, 17 737-200Advs, five 727-100 freighters, six MD-11s, seven DC-10-30s, and two DC-10-30F freighters, plus the aircraft operated by Rio-Sul (*see also* Hong Kong's Cathay Pacific).

Varig (Viação Aérea Rio-Grandense)
Address: Avenida Almirante Silvio de Noronha 365, Rio de Janeiro 20.021-101, Brazil.
Telephone: +55 21 272 5000
Fax: +55 21 272 5700

VASP (Viaçao Aérea de São Paulo) was formed in 1933 and flies an extremely extensive network of routes within Brazil, making it the main domestic operator. It also has international destinations to Aruba, Argentina, the USA, South Korea and Belgium, among others. The current fleet comprises 22 737s, six MD-11s and a DC-10-30, plus three A300B2s.

Other Brazilian scheduled passenger airlines with sizeable aircraft are AirVias with two 727s and a DC-8-62 operating out of São Paulo; InterBrasil Star offering domestic services with a 737-300 and a small fleet of Brasilias but with eight EMB-145 twin-jets on order; Pantanal Linhas Aéreas Sul-Matogrossenses, flying scheduled domestic and international routes within South America with three ATR-42-300s and three Bandeirante/Brasilias; TABA Transportes Aéreos Regionais da Bacia Amazonica with very extensive domestic and regional services using eight Bandeirantes plus ten other aircraft which

OPPOSITE
One of two Air Botswana ATR 42-320s

BELOW
One of six Varig McDonnell Douglas MD-11s

ABOVE
Royal Brunei Airlines Boeing 767-300ER

RIGHT
Royal Air Cambodge ATR 72 prior to delivery

include two Fokker 100 twin-jets and four Dash 8s; and TAM Transportes Aéreos Regionais with a huge domestic/regional network flown with a fleet of 56 aircraft that include 23 Fokker 100s, ten Fokker 50s, up to seven F27s and 22 Cessnas.

Brunei

Negara Brunei Darussalam has three airports handling international scheduled flights. The national airline is Royal Brunei Airlines, founded in 1974. It has a fleet of nine 767-300ERs, two 757-200ERs and two Fokker 50s, which fly to three European destinations (London, Zurich and Frankfurt), four in the Middle East, 14 in the Indian sub-continent and Asia, four in the Orient (Beijing, T'aipei, Osaka and Hong Kong), and three in Australia. The number of employees in August 1996 amounted to 1,700.

During the accounting year 1994-95 the airline carried 787,588 passengers over an accumulated 2,029,602,771 RPK, plus 28,096 tons (28,547 tonnes) of cargo and mail.

Royal Brunei Airlines
Address: PO Box 737, Bandar Seri Begawan 1907, Brunei Darussalam.
Telephone: +673 2 240500
Fax: +673 2 244737

Bulgaria

Balkan Bulgarian Airlines has received some western aircraft and now counts among its fleet three A320s, two 767-200ERs and three 737-400s. The remainder comprises 15 Tu-154Bs, seven Tu-154Ms, five

Tu-134s, 14 An-24s, three An-12 freighters and a quantity of old Il-18s. It offers scheduled and charter flights to destinations in Africa, Asia, Europe, the Middle East, and the USA.

The charter operator, Air Via Bulgarian, also has Sofia as its main base and flies five Tu-154Ms.

Balkan Bulgarian Airlines
Address: Sofia Airport, Sofia 1540,
Bulgaria.
Telephone: +359 2 79321
Fax: +359 2 796169

Burkina Faso

This small African nation with a population of over 10 million has two airports, of which Ouagadougou (the capital) is the main base for the national airline, Air Burkina. Founded in 1967, it has one F28 and one EMB-110 Bandeirante connecting the other airport at Bobo Dioulasso and foreign destinations in Benin, Congo, Mali, Ivory Coast and Togo.

Burundi

Air Burundi is the national airline, operating one or two Twin Otters and a Beech 1900C from the country's only airport for scheduled flights at Bujumbura (the capital), taking in eight regional destinations.

Cambodia

Cambodia has six airports for scheduled flights. The national airline, Royal Air Cambodge, has Phnom Penh as its main base and flies a small fleet of two ATR 72s and two 737-400s, which make scheduled and charter flights to Hong Kong, Malaysia, Singapore, Thailand and Vietnam.

Cameroon

Cameroon Airlines or Camair, operates from Douala in the Littoral province, one of five airports handling scheduled flights. However, it is principally a charter airline serving the region and has a 747-200B Combi for passengers and freight, two 737-200s and a BAe 748. A smaller domestic-only charter airline is Air Affaires Afrique with five aircraft, the largest of which is a Dash 8.

Canada

Canada has well over 50 airlines offering scheduled international and domestic flights, scheduled regional/domestic services, or charter only. Incredibly, there are no fewer than 252 airports handling scheduled operations throughout the huge land mass that makes up the country.

One of the two main airlines is Air Canada, which inaugurated its first service between Vancouver and Seattle using a Lockheed 10A on 1 September 1937 under its original name of Trans-Canada Airlines. Today Air Canada provides scheduled passenger jet services to 17 Canadian cities, 23 cities in the USA and 22 destinations in Europe, the Caribbean, the Middle East and Asia. It also offers charter operations to six international points. During 1995, the airline flew an average of more than 500 flights each day and carried a total of 10.8 million scheduled and charter passengers. Its global network, schedules and customer services are enhanced through strategic alliances with other major airlines, including Lufthansa, Continental Airlines, United Airlines, All Nippon Airways, Korean Air, Cathay Pacific and Swissair. The latest yearly RPK was recorded at 28,815 million.

Air Canada wholly owns the regional airlines AirBC (five BAe 146s and 20 Dash 8-100/300s), Air Ontario (23 Dash 8-100/300s), Air Alliance (nine Dash 8-100s), Air Nova (five BAe 146s and 12 Dash 8-100s) and affiliated Northwest Territorial Airways (three 737 Combis and a Hercules freighter), which together serve 47 Canadian and five US cities using a combined fleet of 78 aircraft and making them the sixth largest regional airline group in the world. Air Canada's cargo division offers a direct service to 120 destinations.

Air Canada employs some 19,500 personnel worldwide. Its fleet (not including regional airlines) comprises nine Boeing 747s (including six Combis), 23 767-200s and six 767-300s, two A340-300s (fleet of six anticipated), 34 A320s, 19 Regional Jets (five more ordered) and 35 DC-9s.

Air Canada
Address: Air Canada Centre 261,
PO Box 14000, St-Laurent, Quebec, Canada H4Y 1H4.
Telephone: +1 514 422 5000
Fax: +1 514 422 5059

Canada's other principal airline is Canadian Airlines International, headquartered in Alberta and operating a very large fleet to some 125 North American points, six Central/South American cities, six cities in Europe, and 13 or more in Asia and the Pacific. It was founded in 1988 by the merger of Canadian Pacific, Eastern Provincial, Pacific Western and Nordair. CAI benefits from alliances with ten foreign airlines, including American Airlines which holds one-third of its shares.

The domestic/regional/commuter carriers CAI wholly owns Canadian Regional Airlines (with 15 F28s, 21 Dash 8s, 12 ATR 42s and two Shorts 360s), Ontario Express, Time Air and other companies, and

has an important holding in Air Atlantic (six Dash 8s, five Jetstream 41s and three BAe 146s). The main CAI fleet comprises 43 737-200s, 11 767-300ERs, four 747-400s, 12 A320-200s and ten DC-10-30s.

Of the many other airlines operating within or from Canada, a sample spread includes the charter carrier Air Club International flying four A310s and two 747-200s; Air Transat offering both scheduled and charter regional/international flights with six TriStars and four 757s; Canada 3000 flying regional/international charters with four A320s and five 757s; First Air operating an extensive scheduled network within Canada and to Greenland (plus charters) with a large fleet of 23 aircraft that includes 727s; the newly formed Greyhound Air for scheduled domestic operations with six 727s; Inter-Canadian, offering scheduled regional/domestic flights with seven ATR 42s and three F28s; Kelowna Flightcraft Air Charter with a range of aircraft that includes 727s and Convair 580s; the charter cargo carrier Morningstar Air Express with 727s and other smaller types; and Royal Airlines for international/regional passenger charters with many large jets including TriStars.

Cape Verde

Cape Verde, an island group off the coast of West Africa, has nine airports handling scheduled flights. The flag carrier is TACV (Transportes Aéreos de Cabo Verde) based at Praia (the capital city) that has a small but busy fleet of two new ATR 42s and two Twin Otters.

Cayman Islands

Founded in 1968, Cayman Airways flies two 737-200s from Georgetown on Grand Cayman to points in Jamaica and the USA.

Chad

Chad (or Tchad) has four airports handling scheduled flights. Air Tchad is the small scheduled and charter domestic/regional airline of this African republic, founded in 1966 and operating a Twin Otter, an F27 and two DC-3s.

Chechnya

This breakaway region of the Russian Federation has its own airline operating regional scheduled and charter services as STIGL, with Tu-134s and An-24s.

Chile

Chile has 18 airports handling scheduled flights. All four of its principal airlines are members of IATA and are based in Santiago. Lan-Chile (Línea Aérea Nacional de Chile) is one of the oldest airlines in the world, having formed in 1929. It is the principal

MAIN PICTURE
Air Canada Airbus A340-300

INSET
Canadian Airlines International Airbus A320-200

LEFT
Air China International's single Boeing 747-200F Freighter

BELOW
One of ten Fokker 100s operated by China Eastern Airlines

OPPOSITE
SAM Colombia Avro International RJ100 prior to delivery, with Lufthansa and Air Malta RJs to the rear

scale. It has also received seven A300s but operates ten (some leased), five A310s (though none were listed by Airbus as operational in August 1996) and three of the eight A340s ordered (two received May and July 1996). Its six large-capacity US-built MD-11s are for limited but important international passenger/cargo services to Bahrain, Belgium, Spain and the USA.

China Northern Airlines, operating out of Shenyang and Shenzhen, was the first airline to operate Chinese-built MD-82s and its current fleet includes 25 of these aircraft. It also has MD-90s on order but the large-capacity element of its fleet comes from five A300-600Rs (of six received).

China Northwest Airlines, headquartered in Xi'an, also has five A300-600s (two leased plus three delivered of six ordered) and three A310s, while among other types can be counted nine Tu-154s and ten BAe 146s. Unlike China Northern, its services encompass some international destinations, to Hong Kong, Japan and Singapore, with Thailand expected to be added.

China Southern Airlines at Guangzhou has 32 737s, 15 757s, six 767s and a small number of 777s as the main aircraft to serve over its regional/domestic network, to which ten A320s will be added.

China Southwest Airlines at Chengdu is the smallest of China's six principal airlines, although it now has a fleet of 13 757-200s and 11 737-300s, plus five Tu-154s among other types.

Although space does not permit examination of many of the smaller Chinese airlines, it is interesting to record that China United Airlines operates as part of the People's Air Force over a network of more than 50 domestic destinations using a 19-aircraft fleet based around eight Tu-154s and four 737s; Shanghai Airlines is to supplement its eight 757/767s by a further six similar aircraft; Sichuan Airlines has three A320s and six Tu-154s among its fleet, and Xiamen Airlines has 12 or more 737/757s to link 31 domestic points plus a service to Hong Kong.

Chilean international/domestic airline, operating to many internal cities and internationally to South American countries, the USA, Germany and Spain. Its most recent acquisitions are some nine 767-200ER/-300ER wide-body jets (some leased), joining a similar number of 737-200s, two BAe 146s and two DC-8-71F freighters. Fast Air Carrier is a charter cargo-carrying subsidiary with three DC-8-71F and 707 freighters.

Lan-Chile
Address: Estado 10, Piso 13,
Casilla 147-D, Santiago, Chile.
Telephone: +56 2 639 4411

The passenger carrier Ladeco (Líneas Aéreas del Cobre SA), which operates to many destinations in the Americas plus some 12 domestic points, has a fleet of two 757-200ERs, 12 737-200/-300s, two 727-100s and four BAC One-Elevens. Its cargo counterpart is Ladeco Cargo. Iberia of Spain has a 38.07 per cent interest in Ladeco.

The newest major Chilean airline is National Airlines (Chile), founded in 1992 and flying four 737-200 Advs.

China
In the late 1980s, the Chinese government decided to break up the state-owned CAAC airline into smaller operating units with their own identities. Air China International became the new name for the element taking over CAAC's international routes and some domestic services from its main operating base at Beijing, while other former CAAC sections specialized in regional/domestic networks. Then, in 1994, the Chinese Government altered its whole policy towards civil air transport, introducing a number of new measures with far reaching effects. These included allowing foreign investment to assist in the development of civil airports and airlines, and abolishing the civil aircraft import licensing system to open up the aviation market. Further, Chuncheng airport in Hainan became the first privately-run airport in China. Presently, China has 108 airports handling scheduled flights.

There are approximately 30 main Chinese

airlines, when including operators with small numbers of locally manufactured twin-turboprop Y7s, though the majority have at least a few pure jets within their fleets. Of these, six are the principal carriers of China. Air China International is the largest and remains government owned (flag carrier). Its fleet encompasses 18 737s, 16 747s and ten 767s, while many more Boeings on order to upgrade the fleet include 13 757s, three 767s, three 747-400s (ordered July 1996) and four 747-400 Combis. Three A340s have also been ordered from Airbus Industrie. To the Boeings currently in use are added a single An-12 and two L-100-30 Commercial Hercules freighters plus six Y7s and four BAe 146s.

Air China International Corporation
Address: Capital International Airport,
Beijing 100621, China.
Telephone: +86 1 456 3220
Fax: +86 1 456 3348

Of the airlines flying over mainly regional/domestic networks, China Eastern Airlines based in Shanghai has a mixed fleet of over 70 aircraft that ranges from some 13 MD-82 twin-jets built in China by Shanghai Aviation (Chinese built MD-90s are on order) to Shijiazhuang Y5 biplanes at the other end of the size

Colombia

Colombia has no fewer than 70 airports. Aérovias Nacionales de Colombia (Avianca) is the main airline and a member of IATA, offering scheduled international services to Argentina, Brazil, Chile, Ecuador, Peru, Venezuela, France, Spain and the USA. Though dating from 1940, the companies that merged in its formation included one of 1919 lineage, giving rise to the claim that Avianca is among the oldest airlines in the world. Its current fleet relies heavily on 11 MD-83s, supplemented by four 767s, three 757s and two older 727s, while the ten Fokker 50 airliners are to be joined by others on order.

Aérovias Nacionales de Colombia (Avianca)
Address: Avenida Eldorado No 93-30,
Bogotà D.C., Colombia.
Telephone: +57 1 4139500 and 4138370
Fax: +57 1 4138716

Sociedad Aeronáutica de Medellin Consolidada (SAM Colombia) is a subsidiary of Avianca and flies international as well as domestic services from Bogotà to destinations in the Americas plus Aruba and Jamaica with a fleet of nine RJ100s plus four Twin Otters and three 727s.

Aerolíneas Centrales de Colombia (ACES Colombia) has a more extensive international and domestic scheduled and charter network, its mainly turboprop fleet headed by six ATR 42s and ten smaller Twin Otters, joined by seven 727 tri-jets.

In addition to the forementioned, there are other smaller airlines flying scheduled regional and domestic services. These include AeroRepública with some 11 DC-9s and 727s; Intercontinental de Aviación with about eight DC-9s in its fleet; and Aerosucre Colombia with a small all-jet fleet that includes two of the surviving ten French-built Caravelles still to be found in this region.

Comoros

The Comoros Islands off the east coast of Africa have a total population of about 545,000 and have four airports providing scheduled flights. Air Comores operates its single F27 Friendship turboprop airliner out of Moroni on Ngazidja, the largest island.

Congo

Congo has five airports handling scheduled flights and two principal airlines. Aero-Service operates about 11 propeller-driven aircraft and two Gulfstream II twin-jets, the former ranging in size from Cessna lightplanes to three C-212 Aviocars and a single leased Fairchild Metro III commuter airliner. Destinations include points in Angola, Gabon and Zaire.

Lina Congo, also using the capital Brazzaville as its main base, has single examples of a F28 Fellowship twin-jet, F27 and Twin Otter twin-turboprops for its small scheduled domestic network.

Costa Rica

This Central American nation with a population of over 3 million and 13 airports for scheduled flights, has San José as its capital, where the national airline Líneas Aéreas Costarricenses (LACSA) has its headquarters. With four A320s and a similar number of 737-200s, it flies internationally to destinations in Colombia, Mexico, Nicaragua, Venezuela and the USA and recorded a passenger-kilometre total of about 1,425 million some years ago. A subsidiary, Servicos Aéreos Nacionales (SANSA), has two Aviocars and a Douglas DC-3 for domestic passenger and cargo operations. A third airline, Aero Costa Rica, has two 737s for regional and domestic use.

Côte d'Ivoire

Air Ivoire has been flying over regional/domestic routes since 1964 and yet, despite being the government-owned flag airline of this small West African nation operating out of the capital Abidjan, it has only one or two Fokker 100 twin-jets and a Beech King Air 200.

Air Afrique, founded in 1961 and also headquartered/based at Abidjan, is actually the international and regional airline of Côte d'Ivoire and ten other West African states (Benin, Burkina Faso, Central African Republic, Chad, Congo, Mali, Mauritania, Niger, Senegal and Togo). The large-capacity element of its fleet comprises five A300s (two leased) and four A310s (one more ordered), joined by a single 737-200C, two 707-320Cs and an An-12 for freighting. Services run to 16 African destinations, 26 in Europe, two in Canada, to Hong Kong, India, Japan, Thailand, and four in the USA. The yearly passenger-kilometres total for Air Afrique from the Côte d'Ivoire standpoint is thought to be well above 201 million.

Croatia

With just four airports handling scheduled flights, Croatia has Croatia Airlines as its principal carrier (member of IATA), which began services from

Zagreb in 1991. Its fleet of nine aircraft includes five 737-200 Adv twin-jets and three ATR 42 turboprop airliners for domestic routes plus international flights to Albania, Austria, Belgium, the Czech Republic, Denmark, France, Germany, Ireland, Italy, the Netherlands, Russia, Switzerland, Turkey, the UK and Yugoslavia.

Croatia Airlines
Address: Savska Cesta 41, 100 Zagreb, Croatia.
Telephone: +385 1 6160018
Fax: +385 1 530475

Cuba

The air transport system of this Caribbean island accumulated nearly 2.4 billion passenger-kilometres in 1993 but a more recent figure has not been received. The flag airline is the nationalized Cubana, an IATA member, based in Havana and linking all or most of the 14 domestic airports handling scheduled flights. Its international network reaches 19 destinations as diverse as Buenos Aires in Argentina, Kingston in Jamaica, Lima in Peru, Moscow in Russia and many European points among others. It is not surprising that the backbone of its fleet comprises over 30 Russian (including Il-62Ms, Il-76MDs, Tu-154B/Ms and Yak-40/42s) as well as 30 Ukrainian (An-24/26s) aircraft, though some eight F27 Friendships are used.

Cubana
Address: Calle 23 No 64 esquina a. P.,
La Rampa, Vedado, Havana, Cuba.
Telephone: +53 7 334 949
Fax: +53 7 334 174

Aero Caribbean operates out of Havana on a network of scheduled and charter passenger/cargo services linking domestic points plus those to regional and South American cities. It has a total of seven An-26s and Yak-40s, but its other aircraft are old Il-18s and Douglas DC-3s.

Cyprus

Cyprus Airways was formed in 1947 by the Cypriot Government, local business interests and British European Airways, though the Government subsequently increased its stake to 80 per cent. It is a major regional carrier offering both scheduled and charter flights throughout Europe and to the Middle East and Gulf region in alliance with partner airlines.

In the latest full year the airline transported 1,218,900 passengers on scheduled flights, giving an RPK total of 2,735.3 million. Cargo accounted for 15,692 tons (15,944 tonnes), while 21,200 passengers were also carried on charter flights. The current fleet of three A310-203s, one A310-204 and eight A320-200s (three leased out) offers a yearly APK total of 4,107.5 million. Twenty-three destinations in Europe (when counting London's Heathrow and Gatwick separately) are joined by Amman, Beirut, Bahrain, Cairo, Damascus, Dubai, Jeddah, Riyadh and Tel Aviv in Africa and the Middle East.

Cyprus Airways
Address: 21 Alkeou Street, Engomi,
PO Box 1903, Nicosia, Cyprus.
Telephone: +357 2 443 054
Fax: +357 2 443 167

A subsidiary of Cyprus Airways is Eurocypria Airlines, which leases three of the parent company's

A320-200s for international and regional passenger and cargo charter flights. The scheduled and charter airline Kibris Turkish Yollari operates out of Ercan in northern Cyprus mainly on a regional/domestic basis but also includes flights to the UK, using two A310s and four 727s.

Czech Republic

While Czech Airlines (CSA) is by far the most important and well-known carrier in the republic, other airlines include the scheduled/charter Air Ostrava, the charter carrier Skoda, the international/regional Terrex Air Group with three 727s, and Topair with commuter aircraft for flights over a small domestic/international network.

Czech Airlines itself can trace its lineage back to 1923, adopting its current name in 1995. In the latest full year it carried 1,476,031 passengers. Sixty-eight per cent of all revenues from air transport resulted from operations over Western and Eastern Europe, with those to North America and the Far East accounting for 22 per cent, with the remainder coming from the Near/Middle East and Northern Africa flights. New co-operation agreements in 1995 with AUA, Malev and Luxair increased available seat capacity, improved flight scheduling and commercial results on flights to Vienna and Budapest, and allowed the commencement of services between Luxembourg and Prague. Other agreements include code sharing with Continental Airlines for co-operation on US routes. The overall seat capacity utilization for the year was 66.6 per cent, while 10,430 tons (10,600 tonnes) of cargo were carried.

Employed staff then stood at 3,916.

Large capacity airliners consist of two A310-300s (214 seats each), joined by two smaller 737-400s, five 737-500s (ten more ordered for delivery from 1997), four Tu-154Ms (136-seat layout), three Tu-134As, four ATR 72-200s and two ATR 42-320s.

Czech Airlines
Address: Airport Praha, Ruzyne,
160 08 Praha 6, Czech Republic.
Telephone: +42 2 334 2557
Fax: +42 2 316 2774

Denmark

Through Det Danske Luftfahrtsselskab (DDL, Danish Airlines), Denmark is one of three nations in the Scandinavian Airlines System consortium (detailed under Sweden). Scandinavian Commuter, headquartered in Denmark and run by the same three operators as SAS itself, has a large fleet of 41 F28 twin-jets and Fokker 50 turboprop airliners with which to fly regional routes in Europe from Copenhagen under its Eurolink service and domestic routes in Norway under Norlink.

Cimber Air Denmark operates eight ATR 42-300s and a single Cessna Citation on domestic services plus a number of routes in Germany, and also undertakes charter flights. Not surprisingly, it co-operates with SAS for its marketing.

Maersk Air was founded in 1969 and is now becoming an all-Boeing airline by replacing its Fokker 50s with 737-500s, while other business

activities include leasing. Domestic services from Copenhagen and Billund link four other cities, while international connections are made to points in Belgium, the Faroe Islands, France, Germany, Norway, the Netherlands, Sweden and the UK. Its total fleet comprises 15 737-300s, up to ten 737-500s (when including the six being delivered to replace existing Fokker 50s; three more ordered in September 1996), and a number of 727-100F freighters for cargo work. Boeing 737-700s are also on order. Subsidiaries of the airline include Maersk Air UK for European services from Birmingham Airport, and the Danish charter airline Star Air which has leased 727 freighters and an F27 for cargo flights on behalf of UPS plus other work.

Other Danish charter airlines include Premiair, founded in 1994 from the former Conair and Scanair (of Sweden) and offering both regional and international passenger/cargo flights with an impressive fleet of six A320s, three A300s and four DC-10s, and Sterling European Airlines which has a small fleet of 727-200s and a 737-200 mainly for holiday charters.

Airlines with smaller-capacity aircraft for scheduled and/or charter services include Ikaros Fly, Muk Air and SUN-AIR of Scandinavia, the latter with nine Jetstream 31s and two Jetstream 41s among its 18-aircraft fleet.

Djibouti

This small republic on the east coast of Africa has a single airport handling scheduled flights. Puntavia Airline de Djibouti has a mixed fleet of four

turboprop L 410s and an Il-18D, plus two 727-200 tri-jets for regional services.

Dominican Republic

The Dominican Republic (with five airports) is well placed as a hub for Caribbean destinations and the Americas, though its airlines remain small. Compañía Dominicana de Aviación, based at the capital Santo Domingo, had a single 727-200 for flights to Aruba and Curaçao in the Lesser Antilles, neighbouring Haiti, Puerto Rico, Venezuela, and Miami and New York in the USA, plus charters within the Caribbean region.

Aerolíneas Dominicanas (Dominar) is a domestic operator with a Dash 8, while Aerochago Airlines has a single Convair 240.

Ecuador

Ecuador has 14 airports and six principal airlines. As its name suggests, Transportes Aéreos Militares Ecuatorianos (TAME) is run as an element of the Air Force, based at the capital Quito, with a fleet of seven 727s and a single F28-4000 Fellowship to fly a domestic network of 14 destinations that includes the Galápagos islands.

From the hub of Guayaquil in the region of Guayas, Aeroservicios Ecuatorianos (AECA) operates as a domestic airline with a 727 freighter, two 707-320B/Cs and two lightplanes. Cargo airlines are Aerolíneas Nacionales del Ecuador (ANDES

Airlines) with a DC-8-50F and Servicios Aéreos Nacionales with a 727.

Until 1993 the national airline of Ecuador was Ecuatoriana, but when services were terminated its routes to the USA were taken over by SAETA. However, with VASP Brazilian Airlines taking a majority shareholding in Ecuatoriana in 1995, the airline was subsequently reinstated for flights within the Americas and to Europe with mostly leased aircraft.

SAETA (Sociedad Ecuatoriana de Transportes Aéreos) itself is a principal airline of Ecuador, offering scheduled operations to Guayaquil plus ten foreign destinations, including Los Angeles, Miami and New York in the USA, as well as charters. It has a fleet of three A320s and two A310s, one 737-200 and two 727s.

ABOVE
One of 22 Fokker 50s operated by Scandinavian Commuter

LEFT
One of two Airbus A310-300s operated by Czech Airlines

Egypt

This nation, with a population of over 56 million, benefits from 14 airports. Its nationalized flag airline is EgyptAir, which has a lineage that can be traced back to 7 June 1932 and the formation of Misr Airwork, becoming Misrair in 1949, United Arab Airlines in 1960 and EgyptAir in 1971.

Employing approximately 5,000 people, EgyptAir's worldwide network of services covers 11 domestic cities, 21 European destinations, the USA, Australia, 24 points in the Middle/Far East and Asia, and 15 throughout Africa. It has established co-operation agreements with a large number of foreign airlines.

In July 1996, EgyptAir's fleet was headed by seven A320s, 14 A300s (of 17 delivered) and an A340 (of three ordered), with four A321s also due for later delivery. To these it adds five 767-200/300 ERs, two 747-300 Combis, nine 737-200/500s and two 707-320Cs, plus two F27 Friendships. Boeing 777s were then awaited.

EgyptAir
Address: Cairo International Airport,
Cairo, Egypt.
Telephone: +20 2 3902444
Fax: +20 2 3901557

Like EgyptAir, Shorouk Air is Cairo-based and a member of IATA. Non-IATA airlines are Air Sinai which offers scheduled flights with two 737s and two F27s and is a subsidiary of EgyptAir; the charter airline AMC Aviation with three 737s; the recently founded Orca Air with two Fairchild Metro 23s; and Transmed Airlines with two 737s. All are based in Cairo with the exception of Orca, which operates from Sharm el Sheikh.

El Salvador

This Central American republic has a single airport for scheduled flights. TACA International Airlines dates from 1931, when the original Honduran-based TACA airline was founded, which subsequently moved its international hub for Central American operations to San Salvador under the guise of TACA El Salvador. Today it is a member of IATA.

TACA continues to fly out of the capital San Salvador to some 15 points in the Americas, including those in Belize, Guatemala, Mexico, Panama and the USA, providing a passenger-kilometre total that a few years ago was estimated at approximately 1,290 million. It has an all-Boeing fleet; two A320s received were not recorded as operational by Airbus in August 1996. As well as two 767-200/300ERs, the airline has ten 737-200/300s.

Equatorial Guinea

A tiny West African republic of some 396,000 population, it has two airports handling scheduled flights. The flag airline is Ecuato Guineana de Aviación, offering both scheduled and charter services with a Vickers Viscount.

Estonia

Estonia has two airports for scheduled flights. The national flag carrier is Estonian Air, offering international/regional services out of Tallinn. A member of IATA, it was formed in 1992 as an independent splinter of Aeroflot (it is now being privatized) and as such has a number of Tu-134s and Yak-40s, though some are being withdrawn as the airline modernizes. It has recently received two leased 737-500s to replace Tu-134s previously used on routes within Europe and it was the first operator of new Boeings within the independent Baltic States. The first 737 was put on the route between Tallinn and Amsterdam, also serving Copenhagen, Frankfurt, Hamburg and Stockholm.

Estonian Air
Address: Lennugaama 2,
EE0011 Tallinn, Estonia.
Telephone: +372 2 219 316
Fax: +372 2 211 624

Elk Estonia Airline has three Tu-154Ms and two L 410s for scheduled and charter flights in Europe, from its base at Tallinn.

Ethiopia

Ethiopian Airlines, the government-owned national carrier, was founded on 30 December 1945, initially with assistance from TWA. Today, 50 years on, it has a staff of 3,253 and a fleet comprising two 767s (a third was lost during a hijacking in November 1996),

four passenger and one all-cargo 757s, one 737, one 707 freighter, two ATR 42s, four DHC-6 Twin Otters, a DHC-5 Buffalo, and two L-100-30 Hercules freighters. In addition, 14 light aircraft are mainly used at the airline's training centre, which provides courses for pilots, maintenance technicians, cabin crew, and marketing and finance personnel. Five Fokker 50s were on order.

The airline flies to 40 international destinations in Africa, Europe, the Middle East and Asia from Addis Ababa, among the latest routes adding New Delhi in July 1995, while its extensive domestic route structure takes in 40 locations. Ethiopian remains the only airline with a daily east-west flight across Africa and serves three routes across the continent. Over two-thirds of its route network is within Africa.

The airline also runs one of the most modern and comprehensive aircraft and engine overhaul and repair facilities in Africa. Under its Agro Aircraft Manufacturing Plant, established in 1986, it also manufactures the Eshet, a version of the Turbo Ag-Cat crop-duster aircraft.

Ethiopian Airlines
Address: PO Box 1755, Addis Ababa, Ethiopia.
Telephone: +251 1 612222
Fax: +251 1 611474

Falkland Islands

Operating out of Stanley Airport, the Falkland Island Government Air Service has six Pilatus Britten-Norman Islanders to carry small numbers of passengers to over 30 domestic points on a non-regular basis, while also undertaking exclusive economic zone sea patrols.

Faroe Islands

Atlantic Airways has a single BAe 146, which it uses to fly a small network of routes to points in Denmark and Iceland.

Fiji

The Republic of Fiji in the Pacific has 13 airports for scheduled flights. The principal airline is Air Pacific, mainly owned by the government but with Qantas holding a small stake. Its current fleet of two 767ERs, a 747-200 and a 737-500 is entirely leased and is to be joined by a further 767-300ER for its services to 12 domestic, regional island group and international destinations, including Australia, Japan, New Zealand, the Solomon Islands, Tonga, Vanuatu and Western Samoa.

Fiji Air is a small domestic airline with an eight propeller-driven aircraft fleet that includes a Chinese Y-12, three Twin Otters and two Bandeirantes, linking ten points.

Sunflower Airlines (founded in 1980 and now Fiji's largest domestic airline), like Air Pacific, is a member of IATA but is more akin to Fiji Air in the type of aircraft it operates. It benefited from taking over some former Fiji Air routes (using Islanders) when these proved unprofitable for Fiji Air's Twin Otters. Now, with four Islanders, three Twin Otters, a Shorts 330, a Beech B65 Queen Air, a Riley Heron and three Cessna lightplanes, it provides daily services to most of its 15 domestic tourism destinations from bases at Nadi, Nausori and Labasa. In the latest full year it carried more than 150,000 passengers.

Sunflower Airlines
Address: PO Box 9452, Nadi Airport, Fiji.
Telephone: +679 723 555
Fax: +679 720 085

Finland

Air Botnia with three Jetstream 31s and two Bandeirantes, Finnaviation with seven Saab 340s, and Karair with six ATR 72s, are all regional/ domestic airlines flying turboprop aircraft, the latter two forming part of the Finnair Group (*see below*).

Finnair is Finland's flag carrier international airline. It was founded in 1923 as Aero O/Y and began operations with a Junkers F 13 on 20 March 1924 carrying mail from Helsinki to Tallinn. It adopted the slogan 'Finnish Air Lines' in about 1946 and took the name Finnair in 1953 for marketing purposes, though it was not made official until June 1968.

ABOVE
Ethiopian Airlines Boeing 767-200ER

LEFT
Estonian Air Boeing 737-500

OPPOSITE, ABOVE
An impression of an EgyptAir Boeing 777-200

29

Today, the Finnair airline forms the principal element of the Finnair Group that also includes travel agency, package tour, hotel and other business interests. Of the Group's 10,300 total personnel, some 7,600 are employed in airline operations.

Finnair's route network covers 45 destinations, with long-haul flights to New York, San Francisco and Toronto in North America and Singapore and Bangkok in the Far East. It flies to Tokyo, Osaka and Beijing non-stop across Siberia. In addition to regular scheduled services, the airline offers charter flights to several points, particularly holiday resorts in the Mediterranean, the Canary Islands, South-East Asia and the Caribbean. It is interesting to note that on 18 February 1996 Finnair celebrated 40 years of flights to Moscow, having been the first Western airline to start up a Moscow connection.

The Group's fleet comprises 55 aircraft, made up of four MD-11s, four DC-10-30s (leased out), 17 MD-82/83s, three MD-87s, 12 DC-9-50s, two A300Bs, six ATR 72s and seven Saab 340s. Four leased 757-200s will join the airline in late 1997. During the latest financial year, the Group's airlines (Finnair, Finnaviation and Karair) carried 5,963,000 passengers, of which 3,262,000 were on international routes, 2,050,000 on domestic and 651,000 on charter. Cargo and mail totalled 133.34 million pounds (60.484 million kg) in weight. RPK for April 1995 to March 1996 was 10,732 million, which included 1,921 million charter and 918 million scheduled domestic.

Finnair

Address: Tietotie 11 A, Helsinki-Vantaa Airport,
PO Box 15, FIN-01053 Finnair, Finland.
Telephone: +358 0 81 881
Fax: +358 0 818 4092

France

France has so many scheduled and charter airlines that space precludes coverage of more than a few. Indeed, even when applying the size of aircraft operated as a useful cut-off point, there remains a substantial number. For example, among IATA members whose operations include scheduled international and/or regional services can be counted Air France, Air Inter Europe, Air Liberté (three A310s, two A300s, ten MD-83s, two DC-10-30s and seven 737s); Air Littoral (one Fokker 100, five Fokker 70s and six Regional Jet twin-jets, plus a large number of turboprop types including many ATR 42/72s); AOM Minerve (21 MD-83s and DC-10s); Compagnie Aérienne Corse Méditerranée (two Fokker 100s and five ATR 72s); Société Nouvelle Europe Aéro Service; and TAT European Airlines (eight ATR 42s, six ATR 72s, 13 Fokker 100s, 13 F28s, two EMB-120s and others).

TAT is France's leading private airline, founded in 1968. It operates scheduled services to 23 domestic points and over four international routes, the latter from Orly/Paris, Marseille and Lyon to London and from Lyon to Rome. TAT's scheduled international services have carried the British Airways brand name since March 1993, while during the summer months the airline operates a seasonal network of services to which Athens and Geneva are added, among other destinations. During the last full year, TAT carried 1.2 million passengers on scheduled flights and employed an average of 1,294 personnel (see British Airways).

An IATA charter airline is Euralair International, having seven 737s and many small business-type jets,

and with two A321s and two A330s on order along with other types.

Non-IATA airlines with scheduled international/regional links include Air Jet (BAe 146s); Brit Air (with 24 aircraft comprising ATR 42s, ATR 72s, Saab 340s and Regional Jets); Corse Air International (six 747s and three 737s, plus a DC-10); and Regional Airlines (over 20 aircraft including Saab 2000s and 340s, ATR 42s and Jetstream Super 31s, with EMB-145s on order). Charter companies include Aéropostale with 18 737s and some 727 freighters for cargo carrying.

Air France is the French flag carrier and is part of Groupe Air France. Its lineage can be traced to 1933 when five airlines merged, one of which had started life as Farman Airlines which in 1919 had undertaken the first-ever cross-Channel airline flight between Paris and London.

Groupe Air France has substantial share interests in many foreign airlines, while shares in

other French operators include more than a 72 per cent holding in Air Inter and a one-fifth share of Aéropostale. Air Inter now carries the temporary name Air Inter Europe, but in 1997 it will be brought fully under the corporate umbrella of Groupe Air France and take the new name Air France Europe. Air Inter Europe operates (in August 1996) 51 Airbus airliners (three A319s, 35 A320s, five A321s, four A300s and four A330s), while a further six A319s, two A321s and ten A330s are on order. In addition, it has five Fokker 100s. As an international and domestic scheduled and charter airline based at Orly, Air Inter Europe flies extensively throughout Europe.

Air France itself uses Charles de Gaulle airport in Paris as its main base. It has a huge fleet, headed by five supersonic Concordes. In July 1996 it had 52 Airbus airliners in operation, represented as 23 A320s (of 26 delivered), ten A310 (of 11 delivered), seven A300s and 11 four-engined A340s. Additional aircraft are 46 747s, 38 737s, eight 767s and a single

DC-10. Apart from flying to 70 destinations in Europe, its worldwide network (with many foreign airline alliances) add over 20 points to North and South America and 68 elsewhere in the world.

Air France
Address: 45 Rue de Paris,
95747 Roisst CDG, France.
Telephone: +33 1 41 56 78 00 or 84 40
Fax: +33 1 41 56 84 39

French Antilles
Air Saint-Barthélemy, Air Guadeloupe and Air Martinique are regional airlines named after their base islands. Between them they fly ATR 42s, Trislanders, Twin Otters and Dornier 228s.

Gabon
Gabon has six airports handling scheduled flights. The national airline is Air Gabon, operating out of the capital Libreville to domestic cities plus some 19 foreign destinations in Africa and further afield, including Britain, France and Italy. In addition to two F28 Fellowships, its fleet comprises a 747 Combi, a 737 and 727Adv. Air Inter Gabon and Air Service Gabon are small domestic airlines.

Georgia
This republic, formerly part of the USSR, has one principal airport offering scheduled flights. As an offshoot of Aeroflot, ORBI Georgian Airlines operates a fleet of 28 Tu-134s, Tu-154Bs and Yak-40s, plus Mi-8 helicopters, from Tbilisi to regional cities plus Egypt and Israel.

A joint venture with Germania has produced the subsidiary ORBI Georgian Airways, with a Brazilian-registered 737-300. Also, Taifun has seven Tu-134s for domestic services.

Germany
Six German airlines are members of IATA. Augsburg Airways (formerly Interot Airways) is a subsidiary of Augsburger, a forwarding agency. Founded in 1980, it commenced regular flights in 1986, with scheduled services starting three years later. In the last full accounting year it employed 150 persons (55 crew) and carried 105,400 passengers over a total revenue distance of 1,686,818 miles (2,714,670 km). Its current fleet stands at six Dash 8-100/300s and a Beech 1900C, with one more Dash 8 to be added soon. Domestic services are to Cologne/Bonn, Düsseldorf, Leipzig-Halle, Berlin and Dresden, while direct flights abroad reach London City Airport and Gdansk/Danzig.

Augsburg Airways
Address: Flughafenstrasse 6,
D-86169 Augsburg, Germany.
Telephone: +49 821 27097-0
Fax: +49 821 27097-66

Conti-Flug at Cologne and Eurowings at Nuremberg are also IATA airlines, the latter having a fleet of over 30 BAe 146s, ATR 42 and ATR 72s for its passenger and freight services to many European destinations. It has also ordered three A319s.

LTU International Airways was founded on 20 October 1955 and also incorporates the subsidiary charter airlines LTU Süd International Airways at Munich and LTE International Airways at Palma de Mallorca in Spain (three Boeing 757-200ERs). The current LTU/LTU Süd fleet comprises six A330-300s, four MD-11s, five 767-300ERs and ten 757-200ERs. During the latest full year LTU carried 6.64 million passengers, accumulating more than 29,937 million RPK. It then had a staff of 2,603. Scheduled domestic services are mainly from Düsseldorf to Munich and Hamburg, while regional/international flights in the summer schedule are to 54 scheduled and 15 charter destinations in Europe, the Americas, North Africa, Asia and the Caribbean.

LTU International Airways
Address: Flughafen, Halle 8,
D-40474 Düsseldorf, Germany.
Telephone: +49 211 9418-08
Fax: +49 211 9418-713

The remaining two German IATA member airlines are Deutsche Lufthansa, Germany's flag carrier, and the related Lufthansa Cargo which is the Lufthansa Group's primary freight carrier with 19 aircraft (three 737-200C/300Cs, 11 747-200B/200Fs and five DC-8Fs). In addition, the Lufthansa Group (57,740 employees) controls the subsidiaries Lufthansa CityLine and Condor Flugdienst, the latter having 31 737/757/767s and five DC-10s for its scheduled and charter services to holiday resorts worldwide (24 new 757-300s are intended for service).

Lufthansa CityLine is the Group's regional carrier, operating aircraft of under 100-seat capacity to link Europe-wide cities from hub bases throughout Germany. In the latest period it achieved the highest traffic growth of the Group, carrying 1,258,128 passengers in the first six months of the year alone. It operates 47 aircraft, including 19 Bombardier Canadair Regional Jets, nine Avro International RJ85s and 14 Fokker 50s.

Deutsche Lufthansa itself was founded in Berlin on 6 January 1926 as Deutsche Luft-Hansa AG, following the merger of Deutsche Aero Lloyd and Junkers Luftverkehr. In 1928 it established the first air cargo service using dedicated freighters and in 1934 became the first airline to provide an air mail service to South America. Its first period of operation was brought to a close, however, with the end of the Second World War, but in 1953 Lufthansa German Airlines was founded in Cologne, starting scheduled services two years later.

At the time of writing, Lufthansa had an operational fleet comprising 101 Boeing 737s, 25 747s, 12 A300s, 11 A310s, two A319s (delivered July and August 1996; 18 more on order), 33 A320s,

ABOVE
Lufthansa Boeing 737-400, one of ten in use

15 A321s (five more on order) and 15 A340s (one more on order). It flies to 213 destinations in 84 countries and in the last full year carried 31,960,000 passengers on some 340,972 flights, accumulating 59,916 million RPK.

Deutsche Lufthansa Aktiengesellschaft (Lufthansa German Airlines)
Address: Von-Gablenz Strasse 2-6,
50679 Cologne, Germany.
Telephone: +49 221 8260
Fax: +49 221 826 3818

Of the many other German airlines, those with fleets of large aircraft include the charter carriers Aero Lloyd Flugreisen, Air Berlin and Germania Fluggesellschaft, as well as the scheduled/charter operators Deutsche BA Luftfahrtgesellschaft, Hamburg Airlines, and Hapag-Lloyd Fluggesellschaft.

Ghana

Ghana Airways was founded on 4 July 1958 in association with BOAC, though British shares were redeemed by the Ghana Government in 1961. In the following year, the BOAC agreement was terminated and the airline became a state corporation. Its current fleet comprises two DC-10-30s (one leased) and a DC-9-50, operating from Accra to ten cities in Africa plus London, Rome, New York and Düsseldorf. A total of 186,605 passengers was flown during the last full year over an accumulated distance of 3,085,571 miles (4,965,745 km), plus 13,177,100 pounds (5,977,040 kg) of cargo.

Ghana Airways Limited
Address: Ghana Airways House,
PO Box 1636, Accra, Ghana.
Telephone: +233 21 773321, 772338, 773329
Fax: +233 21 777078, 777675

Greece

Olympic Airways, the nation's flag carrier, was founded on 6 April 1957 with a fleet of Douglas DC-3s and a DC-4. On 18 May 1960 it introduced de Havilland Comet 4B jet services on its Athens-Rome-London route and all Middle East destinations, while in 1975 all shares and assets held by the Onassis Group were officially taken over by the Government. Although Athens remains its main base, Thessaloniki's Macedonia International Airport became its second hub in March 1996.

Olympic Airways has a domestic network covering 34 cities, while its international routes reach 43 destinations in Europe, Africa and the Middle East, Asia, the Americas and Australia, including new services to Rio de Janeiro and São Paulo in

INSET
Ghana Airways McDonnell Douglas DC-10-30

ABOVE RIGHT
Olympic Airways Boeing 737-400

co-operation with VASP, plus flights from Corfu to Geneva and from Rhodes to Beirut. During the last full year it carried 2,385,000 passengers on domestic services and 2,492,000 internationally. Its fleet comprises six A300B4s, two A300-605Rs, four 747-200Bs, 11 737-284s, seven 737-484s, five 727-200s and a Dassault Falcon 900B.

Olympic Aviation is Olympic Airways' commuter airline, flying domestic and regional services with five Shorts 330s, seven Dornier 228-201s, four ATR 42s, seven ATR 72s and eight lightplanes and helicopters.

Olympic Airways
Address: 96-100 Syngrou Avenue,
117 41 Athens, Greece.
Telephone: +30 1 9269111
Fax: +30 1 9216777

Other airlines include Air Greece with two ATR 72s, and the charter operators Southeast European Airlines (IATA member) with a nine-aircraft fleet that includes two MD-87s; Apollo Airlines with three leased A300s; Cretan Airlines which had three A320s but was not listed as a user in the August 1996 Airbus listings; Cronus Airlines with a 737; and Venus Airlines with a growing fleet that includes seven MD-83/87s.

Greenland

Grønlandsfly, founded in 1960, has six Dash 7s and Twin Otters, a Beech Super King Air and 18 helicopters for its domestic/regional services (see SAS under Sweden).

Grenada

This island off the coast off Venezuela has two airports for scheduled flights. The national carrier is Airlines of Carriacou, with two Islanders for its regional services.

Guam

This US Trust Territory of the Pacific island in the Marianas supports Air Mike Express, operating two F27s to the more northerly islands of Rota and Saipan, and Continental Micronesia.

Founded on 16 May 1968, Continental Micronesia is a US-certified international carrier (IATA member) engaged in transporting passengers, cargo and mail in the Western Pacific. It employs 1,662 persons. It mainly serves five markets from its hubs in Guam and Saipan, namely seven Japanese cities, Asian destinations (including Taiwan, Manila, Hong Kong, South Korea and Bali), the islands of Micronesia and, through its non-stop service to Honolulu, the USA, a route network of 23 destinations. The fleet of 21 aircraft comprises 727-200, DC-10-10, DC-10-30 and 747 types.

Continental Micronesia
Address: PO Box 8778-S,
862 South Marine Drive,
Tamuning, Guam 96931.
Telephone: +1 671 646 0212

Guatemala

Two airports handle scheduled flights. Aerolíneas de Guatemala (Aviateca) flies from Guatemala City to Flores and abroad to 11 destinations in the Americas using five 737-200s. A domestic charter airline with mainly Twin Otters is Aviones Commerciales de Guatemala.

Guinea

This West African country has two main airports for scheduled flights. Air Guinea has a small fleet of four aircraft (An-24, An-26, Dash 7 and 737-200C) for its network to eight domestic and six regional destinations. Also operating out of the capital, Conakry, is Guinée Air Service with two An-26s and lightplanes.

Guinea-Bissau

Another West African country with two airports for scheduled flights. The nationalized airline is TAGB Transportes Aéreos da Guinea-Bissau (Air Bissau), flying domestic services with a BAe 748 turboprop airliner.

Guyana

Founded in 1939, Guyana Airways is a small South American airline offering services to Miami, New York and Toronto from the single airport for international scheduled flights at Georgetown, while an extensive domestic network to more than 20 points is flown on a charter basis. The fleet comprises a 757-200ER, two BAe 748s and two Twin Otters.

Haiti

This Caribbean island has two airports for scheduled flights. Haiti Trans Air flies out of the capital Port-au-Prince on regional flights with one 727-200, though its head office is in Florida.

Honduras

Honduras has eight airports for scheduled flights. Islena Airlines operates a scheduled domestic network with five Bandeirantes, a Shorts 360, a Fairchild FH-227 and two Beech lightplanes.

Hong Kong

Cathay Pacific Airways, Hong Kong's flag carrier, has its origins in the *ad hoc* charter flights undertaken by American Roy Farrell in 1946, who began operating out of Shanghai using a refurbished C-47 but quickly transferred to Kai Tak in Hong Kong. The airline was officially founded in Hong Kong on 24 September 1946 by Farrell and the Australian Sydney de Kantzow, who had previously met while flying C-47s 'over the hump' from Calcutta to China during the Second World War. In 1959 the airline took in its first turbine aircraft, two Lockheed Electras.

Today Cathay Pacific flies to 46 destinations in

27 countries and territories, figures which include a cargo-only service to Chicago and a new passenger service to New York which began in July 1996. During the latest full year it carried 10,381,000 revenue passengers, while in April 1996 alone it transported 943,624 passengers to record a gross passenger load factor of 75.9 per cent. The company then employed 15,038 people.

The Cathay fleet comprises 19 747-400s (two leased in), seven 747-200Bs, six 747-300s, four 747-200 freighters, two 747-400 freighters, 777-200/-300s (eleven ordered, the first 777-200 was delivered on 10 May 1996 and delivery of 777-300s will be from May 1998), seven A340-200s (four leased; three delivered from orders in June/August 1996) and eight A330-300s. It then had 19 aircraft on order (A330-300s, ex-Varig 747-200Fs for lease to Air Hong Kong, and A340-300s), and 32 aircraft on option.

Cathay Pacific Airways
Address: Swire House, 9 Connaught Road, Central, Hong Kong.
Telephone: +852 2747 5000
Fax: +852 2810 6563

Hong Kong Dragon Airlines, generally known as Dragonair, was founded in April 1985. Cathay Pacific and the Swire Group (Cathay's parent company) now own 43 per cent of the issued share capital. It currently operates to 14 cities in China and eight other destinations in Bangladesh, Cambodia, Japan, Malaysia and Thailand with a fleet of seven A320s and four A330s. It carried 1,655,000 passengers in the latest full year.

Hong Kong Dragon Airlines
Address: 22/F, Devon House, Taikoo Place, 979 King's Road, Quarry Bay, Hong Kong.
Telephone: +852 2590 1328
Fax: +852 2590 1333

Air Hong Kong is a non-IATA airline, with Cathay Pacific holding the majority of its shares. It operates two 747-200s for scheduled/charter flights to international destinations.

Hungary
Malev Hungarian Airlines is Hungary's flag carrier and a member of IATA. Founded in 1946, it took its present name in 1954 and was privatized in 1992 (Alitalia now holds 30 per cent of the share capital). Other changes have come with the arrival of more Boeing jets and a modern livery. Operating out of Budapest, Hungary's only airport for scheduled flights, it flies scheduled and charter services to 44 foreign destinations, mainly in Europe and the Middle East. Its fleet comprises five Russian-built Tu-154s and three Tu-134s, plus two 767-200ERs, 12 737s and four Fokker 70s.

Malev Hungarian Airlines
Address: Vorosmarty ter 5, 1051 Budapest, Hungary.
Telephone: +36 1 266 3785
Fax: +36 1 266 9946

Iceland
Iceland is thought to have 24 airports handling scheduled flights. Icelandair, as the flag carrier, was founded in 1973 as a result of the merger of two airlines (Flugfélag Islands, founded in 1937, and Loftleidir that was founded in 1944). In the latest full

year, Icelandair carried 830,124 passengers on international routes, 266,784 on domestic services, and 35,221 on international charter flights, representing an increase of 7 per cent compared with the previous year. It also carried 15,840 tons (16,094 tonnes) of cargo. It has a number of alliance agreements with other companies, including code sharing and marketing with SAS, marketing with USAir, and code sharing with LTU to two German destinations.

Its fleet is among the youngest in the world, averaging just four years old. This comprises four 757-200ERs for transatlantic routes between Europe and six gateways in the USA and Canada, four 737-400s serving 18 scheduled European routes and for charter operations, and four Fokker 50s serving nine domestic routes and also for flights to Greenland and the Faroe Islands. The hub is at Keflavik Airport, Iceland's main airport at the capital Reykjavík. Some 1,361 persons are employed.

Icelandair
Address: Reykjavík Airport, 101 Reykjavík, Iceland.
Telephone: +354 5050 300
Fax: +354 5050 350

An important airline flying between 11 international points is Air Atlantic Icelandic, its fleet encompassing six 747s, three TriStars and two 737s. Islandsflug operates three Dornier 228s and other aircraft on scheduled domestic services.

TOP
Hong Kong Dragon Airlines Airbus A320

ABOVE
Icelandair Boeing 757-200ER

OPPOSITE,
TOP
Continental Micronesia Boeing 727-200

OPPOSITE,
BELOW
Cathay Pacific Airbus A330-300 in the airline's new livery

LEFT
Merpati's ninety or more aircraft include five Jetstream ATPs

BELOW
Thirty-three-seat Dornier 328, operated by Hyderabad-based VIF Airways for regional flights

BOTTOM
Air-India Boeing 747-300 Combi

OPPOSITE, TOP
One of 30 Indian Airlines Airbus A320s (an A320-231)

OPPOSITE, BELOW
Boeing 737 belonging to Sahara India Airlines

India

This huge nation of well over 1.2 million sq miles (3.1 million sq km) has 66 airports for scheduled flights. In addition to Air-India and the five Indian IATA-member airlines, it has many domestic/regional operators offering scheduled and/or charter services that include Archana Airways, Continental Aviation, Elbee Airlines, Goa Way, Guajarat Airways, Jagson Airlines, Rajair and UP Air, plus what was the first Indian regional airline, VIF Airways. Also important is the new Lufthansa Cargo India, for international cargo operations.

Air-India is the national flag carrier, though it is not an IATA member. Its international route network, spanning 48 cities in five continents, is served by a fleet of four 747-400s, two 747-300 Combis, nine 747-200s, eight A310-300s, three A300B4s and two wet-leased TriStars, while in November 1996 capacity was to be complemented by two extra 747-400s. In the year ending March 1996, the airline carried 2.7 million passengers.

Air-India was born out of Tata Airlines, which undertook the first scheduled air service in India (carrying mail) on 15 October 1932 using a de Havilland Puss Moth lightplane to fly from Karachi to Mumbai. The introduction of the (British) Empire Airmail Scheme in 1938 led to further expansion. On 29 July 1946 the airline became a public limited company and was renamed Air-India. Later, on 8 March 1948, Air-India International was founded and began flights to London via Cairo and Geneva that June. Nationalization of air transport in India followed in the 1950s, with Indian Airlines being established by merger (see next paragraph), while Air-India International became the overseas airline, the title 'International' being dropped in 1962.

Air-India
Address: Air-India Building, Nariman Point, Bombay 400 021, India.
Telephone: +91 22 202 4142
Fax: +91 22 204 8521

As noted above, Indian Airlines came into being in August 1953 by Act of Parliament, following the merger of eight private airlines. In 1976 it became the

first domestic airline in the world to introduce the wide-bodied A300 airliner. Besides maintenance of its own fleet, it undertakes outside work. Also, its Central Training Establishment trains pilots, cabin crew, engineers and other personnel for its own benefit and that of other airlines.

Indian Airlines has a fleet of 56 aircraft, comprising ten A300s, 30 A320s (of 31 delivered) and 16 737s. However, its subsidiary Alliance Air operates the 737s. Indian Airlines undertakes 220 flights daily to domestic and international destinations. The 51 domestic points include Port Blair in the island of Anadamans and it has 17 international destinations in the Gulf, South-East Asia and South Asia. It carried 8 million passengers in the year 1995-96, over a route network of 73,320 miles (118,000 km), with a seat-load factor of 80 per cent.

Indian Airlines Limited
Address: Airlines House,
113 Gurudwara Rakabanj Road,
New Delhi 110001, India.
Telephone: +91 11 3718951
Fax: +91 11 3711730

East West Airlines, operating domestic flights out of Bombay, has a fleet of ten 737-200s, to be joined by two 737-400s plus leased 737s.

Jet Airways was launched as a domestic airline on 5 May 1993, receiving significant commercial and technical support from its equity partners, Gulf Air and Kuwait Airways. Under an agreement concluded with Malaysia Airlines System, technical and flying training is provided at Kuala Lumpur. It has a leased fleet of four 737-300s and seven 737-400s. Since its launch, it has carried over 3.5 million passengers and now achieves an 82 per cent seat-load factor, reaching 17 Indian cities (including the new points of Vadodara, Jaipur and Thiruvananthapuram).

Jet Airways
Address: C-28 Prem House, Connaught Circus,
New Delhi 110 001, India.
Telephone: +91 11 3312760
Fax: +91 11 3715943

ModiLuft was one of the first scheduled private airlines in India, founded in 1993, and flies to a large number of domestic tourist destinations. Established with the support of Lufthansa, which also provides

technical training and maintenance, it has seven 737-200/-400s to operate 50 flights a day to 22 destinations from its main hub in New Delhi and sub-hubs in Bombay and Calcutta. Yearly passenger total is about 1.8 million.

ModiLuft Ltd
Address: ModiLuft House, A-19, Kailash Colony,
New Delhi 110 048, India.
Telephone: +91 11 6430689
Fax: +91 11 6430929

NEPC Airlines started in 1994 as a feeder route airline and, with the takeover of Damania Airways in 1995 (now known as Skyline NEPC Ltd.), it is the largest private airline in India, covering over 50 destinations. It has a fleet of four 737s that operate primarily on trunk routes for Skyline NEPC, and nine Fokker F27s that fly feeder routes networking India. Customized charter services are offered using two Beech King Air C-90s, though all aircraft in the fleet are available for charter.

Skyline NEPC Ltd
Address: Lyka Labs Building, 77 Nehru Road,
Vile Parie (E), Bombay 400 099, India.
Telephone: +91 22 610 7356
Fax: +91 22 610 7599

Sahara India Airlines is a scheduled domestic operator with two 737-400s and a 737-200, with plans to take in two 737-300s, five ATR 42-500s for feeder services, and seven Eurocopter helicopters during 1996-97. Founded in 1991 but with services not commencing until late 1993, it flies to 11 Indian cities from its hub in Delhi. During the latest full year it carried 365,002 passengers, accumulating 5,128,031 passenger-kilometres; from January to April 1996 alone it flew 108,342 passengers. It has interline agreements with 21 Indian and foreign airlines.

Sahara India Airlines
Address: 7th Floor, Ambadeep,
14 K G Marg, New Delhi 110 001, India.
Telephone: +91 11 332 6851
Fax: +91 11 332 6858

Indonesia
Three Indonesian Airlines are members of IATA, namely the national airline Garuda Indonesia Airways, Garuda's subsidiary Merpati Nusantara Airlines which undertakes flights to a huge number of domestic/regional points, and Sempati Air.

Founded in 1950, Garuda offers scheduled domestic flights to 30 or more locations and international scheduled flights to some 36 destinations in Asia, Australia, New Zealand, the Middle East, the USA and Europe from its main hubs at Denpasar in Bali and Jakarta in Java. It operates 13 A300s, nine 747s, 15 737s, six MD-11s and five DC-10s (six 777-200s and 17 737-300/-500s were ordered on 25 June 1996, with the 737s to be delivered during 1997-99 and the 777s during 2000-2002; nine A330s are also on order).

Garuda Indonesia Airways
Address: Garuda Indonesia Building,
13 Jalan Merdeka Selatan, 10110 Jakarta, Indonesia.
Telephone: +62 21 2310545
Fax: +62 21 2311962

Sempati Air was established as a charter airline in 1968 under the name Sempati Air Transport and is currently Indonesia's largest private airline. When the Government deregulated the air transport industry in 1990, by permitting privately-owned airlines to operate pure-jet aircraft, it became the first private scheduled operator, serving mainly domestic routes. Today Sempati operates from Cengkareng Airport in Jakarta and Surabaya (its main hubs) over a network across the archipelago, serving 24 domestic and five international destinations (Kuala Lumpur, Penang, Singapore, T'aipei and Perth).

On 2 April 1996 the Board of Commissioners agreed to sell 40 per cent of Sempati shares to Asean Aviation Inc., which is now the largest shareholder. The Sempati fleet comprises seven 737s, four A300B4s, seven Fokker 100s, five F27s and two Fokker 70s. The estimated available seat-miles is 2,699,000 (4,343,600 seat-km).

PT Sempati Air
Address: Ground Floor, Terminal Building,
Halim Perdanakusuma Airport,
Jakarta 13610, Indonesia.
Telephone: +62 21 8011612, 809612
Fax: +62 21 8094420, 8011072

Iran
Iran has some 20 airports for scheduled flights. The national airline is Iran Air with a lineage that can be traced to 1946, though it came into being in its own right in 1962, following the merger of two private airlines, Iranian Airways and Persian Air Services.

Operating out of Tehràn to 23 domestic points and 32 international destinations in the Near and Middle East, Europe and Asia, it has a fleet of seven A300s, eight 747s (including a freighter), three 737s, seven 727s and six Fokker 100s. A charter subsidiary is Iran Air Tours.

Iraq
Iraq has not undertaken scheduled air services since mid-1992. The national airline is Iraqi Airways, founded in 1945 as a subsidiary of the state railways and has a potential fleet of well over 70 passenger and cargo aircraft, including 30 Il-76s. A contract for five A310s has been suspended.

1961, when a 707 flew the New York route.

Presently, El Al operates an international network to 50 destinations in Europe, the USA, Canada, Asia and Africa, and is the 25th largest commercial airline in terms of ton/kilometres flown. In 1994 (the latest figures provided) it carried 2,477 million passengers.

El Al's fleet comprises ten 747-200s, three 747-400s, four 767s and five 757s, while it also owns two 737s and two 757s leased to Arkia, Israel's charter airline.

El Al Israel Airlines
Address: Ben-Gurion Airport, Israel 70100.
Telephone: +972 3 9716111
Fax: +972 3 9721442

Ireland

The national airline of Ireland is Aer Lingus, founded on 22 May 1936 and initially operating across the Irish Sea in conjuction with its temporary associate Blackpool and West Coast Air Services, under the joint name Irish Sea Airways. The year 1940 was an important milestone date, when Aer Lingus moved to the newly completed Dublin Airport.

Presently, Aer Lingus has a fleet of four A330s, eight 737-500s and five 737-400s, mostly leased. In addition to seven domestic points, the airline flies to 21 European destinations, while the subsidiary Aer Lingus Shannon adds New York and Boston in the USA and shares the fleet. Another subsidiary is Aer Lingus Commuter, linking points in Ireland and Britain.

Aer Lingus
Address: Dublin Airport, PO Box 180, Dublin, Ireland.
Telephone: +353 1 705 2358, 2222
Fax: +353 1 705 3855

The other IATA airlines are City Jet with two BAe 146s for domestic/regional scheduled services, and Ryanair. Celebrating its 10th anniversary in 1995, Ryanair was Ireland's first wholly independent airline. With a fleet of 11 737-200Advs, it links Ireland to points in Britain, while also offering charters to mainland Europe, and is the biggest passenger carrier on the Dublin-London route (up to 35 flights daily). In total, it offers up to 75 flights a day on nine scheduled routes. In the latest full year it carried over 2.25 million passengers and employed 600 people.

Ryanair
Address: Dublin Airport, County Dublin, Ireland.
Telephone: +353 1 844 4400
Fax: +353 1 844 4402

TransLift Airways flies two A300s and two A320s on mainly tour routes in Europe, while Aer Turas Teo is a cargo airline with two DC-8-63Fs.

Israel

El Al Israel Airlines was established in 1949 as the national airline, flying its first scheduled commercial services to Rome and Paris that August. Earlier than this, however, in September 1948, the airline's non-commercial inaugural flight had carried the country's first President, Chaim Weizman, from Geneva. Using Lockheed Constellations, El Al began flying to North America in 1950 and in October 1957 started turboprop-powered Britannia operations on its Tel Aviv-Munich route. Pure-jet services began in May

ABOVE
Aer Lingus Airbus A330-300. The airline leases three of the four A330s it operates

BELOW
El Al Israel Airlines Boeing 747-400

OPPOSITE, ABOVE
One of fourteen Alitalia Airbus A321s

INSET
Ryanair Boeing 737-200 Adv

Italy

Alitalia is Italy's national airline, over 89 per cent of its shares being held by the Government through a holding company. Founded in 1946 and taking its current name in 1957, it flies to 28 domestic cities and has a vast international network reaching 41 destinations in Europe, nine in Central and South America, five in the USA, two in Canada, nine in Africa, eight in the Middle East, nine in Asia and two in Australia.

The Alitalia fleet is heavily dependent on Airbus airliners, having 14 A300s in service (six leased) and 14 A321s (26 more on order). The remainder of the fleet comprises a staggering 90 MD-82s, eight MD-11s, 14 DC-9s, four 767-300s (leased), and 13 747s which include a pure freighter and five Combis for mixed loads of passengers and freight.

Avianova is a subsidiary of Alitalia, flying many European connections with a fleet of 15 Fokker 70s and numbers of ATR 42/72s. The Fokkers were ordered by Alitalia for Avianova use, with the first delivered on 6 December 1995 and all to be received by 1997.

Meridiana, Italy's largest privately owned airline, was founded as Alisarda in March 1963 and had been intended to assist in the development of tourism along the north-east coast of Sardinia. Its route network and fleet expanded rapidly, surpassing the million passenger mark in 1981 by carrying 1,015,000 persons. In 1990, Alisarda obtained Government authorization to operate domestic services from Rome to Milan-Malpensa Airport, Venice, Palermo and Catania, and from Verona to Naples and Palermo. The decision to change the airline's name to Meridiana was taken in 1991, while also expanding throughout Europe from the Florence and Verona hubs.

During the latest full year Meridiana carried 2,522,119 passengers, of which 2,197,000 were on domestic services. The average load factor was 56 per cent. Its workforce then stood at 1,546 persons. Its current fleet comprises eight MD-82s, six DC-9-51s and four BAe 146-200s. In addition to linking 17 domestic cities, it flies to Frankfurt, Geneva, London, Munich, Nice, Paris, Zurich, Barcelona, Madrid, Parigi and Amsterdam.

Alitalia (Linee Aeree Italiane SpA)
Address: Viale Alessandro Marchetti 111,
00148 Rome, Italy.
Telephone: +39 6 656 22833
Fax: ı30 6 656 24416

Meridiana SpA
Address: Zona Industriale A,
07026 Olbia (Sassari), Sardegna, Italy.
Telephone: +39 789 52600
Fax: ı30 780 23661

Jamaica

This Caribbean island has four airports for scheduled flights. The flag carrier is Air Jamaica, founded in 1968 but since 1994 a private airline, though the Government has interests in the holding company. With a fleet of five A310s, four A300s (four A320s on order) and four 727-200s, it flies to Grand Cayman, London, Nassau and seven cities in the USA from its hubs at Kingston and Montego Bay. Air Jamaica also has a majority share interest in Air Jamaica Express, the domestic airline with three Dornier 228s and an ATR 42.

Japan

The largest passenger airline in Japan today and the world's eighth largest in terms of passengers carried, All Nippon Airways (ANA) was founded in 1952 as Nippon Helicopter & Aeroplane Transport Co. In December 1957 Nippon Helicopter and Far East Airlines merged to form ANA, which began international scheduled passenger services in 1986. In the year ending 31 March 1996, ANA carried 37,615,311 passengers (35,322,171 on domestic routes alone) and some 487,180 tons (495,000 tonnes) of freight.

With a staff of 14,200 and a fleet of 125 aircraft, ANA initiates over 500 flights a day linking 33 Japanese cities which, together with its domestic subsidiary Air Nippon (ANK), represents over half of all passenger traffic in Japan. Internationally, ANA operates 36 routes to 22 cities worldwide, its European network alone taking in London, Paris, Vienna, Frankfurt, Rome and Moscow, with new routes anticipated.

The ANA fleet comprises 18 747-400s, six 747-LRs, 14 747-SRs, two 777-200s, 38 767-300s, 25 767-200s and 21 A320-200s, while 44 aircraft on order include ten 777-300s, seven A321-100s and five A340s.

All Nippon Airways

Address: Kasumigaseki Building,
3-2-5 Kasumigaseki, Chiyoda-ku,
100 Tokyo, Japan.
Telephone: +81 3 3592 3035
Fax: +81 3 3592 3039

Japan Airlines (JAL) is the flag airline, founded in 1953 but now fully privatized. In addition to a domestic network reaching 21 cities from Tokyo, it operates to over 40 international destinations in all continents, including ten in Europe. Its fleet of well over 120 aircraft includes 20 767-300s and 80 747s (including freighters), with the remainder made up of MD-11/DC-10s, 737s and newly delivered 777s (JAL

ordered ten 777-200s and five 777-300s, with the first handed over on 16 February 1996). Some aircraft are leased out to subsidiary airlines, such as Japan Air Charter, Japan Asia Airways and Japan TransOcean Air.

Japan Airlines

Address: Tokyo Building, 2-7-3 Marunouchi, Chiyoda-ku,
100 Tokyo, Japan.
Telephone: +81 3 3284 2100
Fax: +81 3 3284 2120

Japan Air System has an extensive scheduled domestic network plus some 15 established international charter routes. Its fleet includes 34 A300s (the latest A300-600R was delivered on 7 June 1996), 36 MD-80s and various other aircraft which encompass a small number of older NAMC YS-11 turboprop types. YS-11s can also be found with Saab 340s in the fleet of the subsidiary scheduled domestic airline, Japan Air Commuter.

Nippon Cargo Airlines (NCA), like All Nippon, Japan Airlines and Japan Air System, is an IATA member. It was established on 21 September 1978 by the joint investment of four major sealines, as Japan's first and only international all-cargo scheduled and charter airline. It inaugurated a Tokyo-San Francisco-New York service in May 1985, and in November 1995 added its latest route linking Osaka-Chicago-New York.

Employing 635 persons in April 1996, NCA has a fleet of six 747-200Fs and a 747-100F. These serve 13 major destinations in North America, Asia and Europe, namely San Francisco, New York, Chicago, Los Angeles, Hong Kong, Singapore, Bangkok, Seoul, Amsterdam, Milan, Frankfurt, Osaka and Kuala Lumpur.

Nippon Cargo Airlines

Address: Shiroyama JT Mori Building 14F,
4-3-1 Toranomon, Minato-ku, Tokyo, Japan.
Telephone: +81 3 5401 4803
Fax: +81 3 5401 4807

ABOVE
Japan Airlines Boeing 777

LEFT
Air Jamaica Airbus A300 in the airline's new livery

INSET
All Nippon Airways Airbus A320

most modern and best-equipped aeronautical engineering maintenance facilities in Africa at Embakasi, offering its services to other airlines.

Domestic operations comprise over 60 weekly flights between Nairobi and the coastal towns of Mombasa and Malindi, plus daily flights to Kisumu on the shore of Lake Victoria. Regionally, it flies to Harare, Kigali, Lusaka, Lilongwe, Bujumbura, Johannesburg, Addis Ababa, Entebbe, Dar-es-Salaam, Khartoum and Cairo, as well as to the Indian Ocean islands of the Seychelles, and Zanzibar. Other international routes take in seven major European cities, with flights to the East connecting Bombay, Karachi, Dubai and Jeddah.

With a staff of about 2,400 in mid-1996, including 108 flight crew, the airline was equipped in 1996 with three A310-300s (one leased from ILFC), two 737-200s (leased from GPA) and three Fokker 50s. It ordered two 737-300s in July 1996 for 1997 delivery, and has two options on similar aircraft. In 1995/96 it carried 740,000 passengers, accumulating 1,757 million RPK from 2,632 million APK.

Jordan

Royal Jordanian Airlines was established as the national carrier by Royal Decree on 8 December 1963, beginning services with a DC-7 and two Handley Page Heralds offered by the Air Force. By 1992, the airline's passenger and cargo route network took in 49 cities in four continents, offering 112,750 unduplicated route miles (181,455 km) and extending as far as Jakarta in the Far East and Chicago in the West. However, Baghdad, Belgrade and Tripoli were subsequently suspended.

In 1996, its fleet was headed by six A310s and three A320s, serving with older aircraft that comprised of up to five TriStars and three 707F freighters, the two 727-200As having been replaced by A320s on regional and short-haul routes. The airline's cargo facilities have been designed to handle up to 430,000 tons (436,900 tonnes) of air cargo by the year 2000. A subsidiary is Arab Wings, the Arab world's first executive jet charter company.

Royal Jordanian Airlines
Address: PO Box 302, Amman, Jordan.
Telephone: +962 6 672872

Kazakhstan

This large republic was formerly part of the USSR and has six airports handling scheduled international flights, plus others for domestic services only. The principal airline is Kazair, or Kazakhstan National Airways to give it its full title, which has around 30,000 staff and a fleet of approximately 100 aircraft, headed by several new 767-300s, seven Il-86s, 29 Yak-40s, five Yak-42Ds and over 20 An-24s.

Other Kazakhstan airlines are small, though Sayakhat requires special mention for having six Il-76TDs for its domestic and international charter cargo services.

Kenya

Kenya Airways was founded in February 1977 as the nation's flag carrier, following the collapse of East African Airways. Recently privatized, 26 per cent of the airline was acquired by KLM in January 1996. It fully owns the subsidiary Kenya Air Freight Handling Limited that operates an independent freighting business. Kenya Airways has one of the

Other airlines based in Kenya with small fleets of large-sized aircraft are African Airlines International and African Safari Airways, while Airkenya operates many small-capacity aircraft and African Eagle has an ATR and several other types.

Kiribati

This island group in the Pacific Ocean has a tiny population served by 18 airports handling scheduled flights. Air Tungaru is the national domestic carrier, with two Trislanders, two Islanders and a C-212.

Komi

A federal republic within the Russian Federation,

Komi has Komavia as its principal airline, which has a large fleet of Tu-134s plus numerous Antonovs, Yak-40s and Mil helicopters for domestic and international charter operations.

Korea, North

Air Koryo, as North Korea's national airline, was established in 1955 and operates out of the capital P'yongyang, where the only airport handling scheduled flights is to be found. In addition to four large passenger-carrying Tu-154s and six Il-62s, plus two Il-76TDs for heavy freighting, the airline has eight An-24s and a number of old Tu-134s and Il-18s. With destinations as far afield as Beijing and Moscow, the yearly passenger-kilometre total is believed to be in the region of 84 million.

Korea, South

A member of IATA, Korean Air was founded in 1962 and is one of the largest users of Airbus A300s, operating 35 by September 1996. In addition, nine A330s were then on order. The remainder of its fleet then comprised 37 747s, 13 or more MD-80 types, five MD-11s and 12 Fokker 100s, with further 747s, MD-80s and 777s on order.

Flying out of Seoul, its route network takes in ten domestic cities, 25 points in Asia and the Pacific, four in the Middle East, ten in the Americas and eight in Europe. It also founded an aerospace division in 1976 which manufactures aeroplanes and helicopters, produces components for Airbus, Boeing and McDonnell Douglas airliners, and has developed its own lightplane as the Chang-Gong 91.

Korean Air
Address: 41-3 Seosomungdong Choonggu,
100-608 Seoul, Republic of Korea.
Telephone: +82 2 751 7092
Fax: +82 2 751 7386

Asiana Airlines operates to 11 domestic and 18 international cities with a fleet of around 40 Boeing airliners, while Seoul Air International has Jetstreams for domestic and regional charter work.

Kuwait

Kuwait National Airways Company was founded in March 1954 with DC-3s to operate between Beirut, Jerusalem, Damascus and Abadan. It changed its name to Kuwait Airways Corporation in the following year when the Government bought a 50 per cent stake, and in 1962 a de Havilland Comet 4C became its first pure jet.

Following the Gulf conflict, the airline was relaunched as Kuwait Airways, in 1991, and the subsidiary ALAFCO was established as an airline lease and finance company. In July 1996, Kuwait Airways operated five or six A300-600s, three A310s, three A320s and four A340s, together with Boeing 747-200s. The receipt of two 777s in 1998 will enable the fleet to be set at 19 aircraft, while a route network to some 46 countries is being re-established.

Kuwait Airways
Address: Kuwait International Airport,
PO Box 394 Safat, 13004 Safat, Kuwait.
Telephone: +965 434 5555
Fax: +965 431 4726

Kyrgyzstan

With two airports for scheduled flights, the Kyrgyz Republic has Kyrgyzstan Aba Yoldoru as its national airline, headquartered at the capital Bishkek. Evolved from the regional division of Aeroflot and retaining important business connections, its fleet of over 40 aircraft comprises mainly Yak-40s but also includes 14 Tu-154B/Ms and six Tu-134s. A charter airline is Asian Star, with two Tu-154Ms.

Laos

Founded as the national airline in 1991, Lao Aviation operates two leased 737s and two leased ATR 42s, joined by Chinese Y7s and Y-12s for its domestic and regional services.

Latvia

Trading under the name airBaltic, this national airline of Latvia started scheduled operations on 1 October 1995 with management assistance from SAS (a 28.51 per cent shareholder), using two wet-leased Boeing 727-100s from Baltic International USA and crews and technicians provided by Baltic International Airlines (the latter's own operations ceasing in October 1995).

AirBaltic has 190 employees, including 30 pilots, and during January-May 1996 accumulated 23,744,000 RPK. The first aircraft of its own was a leased Saab 340A, which is used on services to Helsinki, Minsk, Tallinn, Vilnius and Warsaw, now joined by three RJ70s leased from Trident Jet Leasing (Ireland) and received in 1996 for flights to Copenhagen, Frankfurt, Geneva, Helsinki, Kiev, London and Stockholm. Connections to Moscow and St Petersburg were then anticipated.

Air Baltic Corporation (airBaltic)
Address: Riga International Airport,
LV1053, Riga, Latvia.
Telephone: +371 7207069, 7207360
Fax: +371 7207369

Of several other Latvian airlines, Riair (Riga Airlines) has a 737-200 for European scheduled passenger services and uses the Saab 340 for its Express operations, while Inversija has four Il-76s and an An-26 for freight carrying.

Lebanon

Middle East Airlines (MEA-Airliban), operating out of Lebanon's only airport for scheduled flights at Beirut, was founded in 1945. With a fleet headed by five A310s and five 747s, it has a route network connecting over 40 cities in the Middle East, Africa, Europe and the Americas, recording a yearly passenger-kilometre total of about 1,588 million.

Trans Mediterranean Airways has four or more 707-320Cs for its international scheduled and charter services.

Lesotho

Lesotho Airways Corporation is an IATA member and has two Twin Otters and an F27 for its services from the capital Maseru to six domestic destinations plus two points in South Africa.

LEFT
Korean Air Fokker 100

INSET
Air Mauritius tail markings (see Page 46)

OPPOSITE,
ABOVE
One of three Fokker 50s used by Kenya Airways

Libya

Libya has 12 airports handling scheduled flights. Libyan Arab Airlines, founded in 1964, carries about 1,260,000 passenger a year. With international flights recently suspended, its usual services to Europe, Africa, the Middle East and Asia have been temporarily curtailed and the airline relies upon its scheduled domestic operations. Its fleet of over 60 large and small aircraft includes some 20 Il-76s, ten 727s and 15 F27s.

Jamahiriya Libyan Arab Airlines
Address: PO Box 2555, Haiti Street,
Tripoli, Libya.
Telephone: +218 21 608860, 602090
Fax: +218 22 30970

Lithuania

The national airline is IATA member Lithuanian Airlines, which in 1991 underwent reform to allow it to compete over new western European routes. As part of this transformation, new aircraft had to be acquired and staff retrained, while its Yak-42Ds were assigned for refurbishment. Other existing Russian/Ukrainian aircraft (Yak-40s, An-24s, An-26s, An-2s and Kamov Ka-26s) were sold, and the remaining Tu-134As and Yak-42Ds will also be sold eventually. Thus, in 1996, the fleet comprises two Boeing 737-200s, six Yak-42Ds and five other Yak-42s, one JetStar 731 and five Tu-134As.

Routes from the hub at Vilnius are to Amsterdam, Berlin, Budapest, Copenhagen, Dubai via Larnaca, Düsseldorf, Frankfurt/Main, Istanbul, London, Madrid, Moscow, Munich, Paris, Rome, Stockholm, Stuttgart, Warsaw and Palanga.

Lithuanian Airlines
Address: A. Gustaicio G.4, 2038 Vilnius, Lithuania.
Telephone: +370 2 630116
Fax: +370 2 266828

Air Lithuania is also Government owned and operates Yak-40s and a Tu-134A on European scheduled and charter services from its hub at Kaunas.

Luxembourg

IATA member Luxair is the flag airline. With a fleet of four 737-400/500s, four Fokker 50s and three Brasilias, it flies to some 33 destinations, mainly in Europe, but including the holiday points of Gran Canaria, Ibiza and others within its scheduled, inclusive tour and charter operations. It also has a substantial shareholding in Cargolux Airlines International, the scheduled and charter airline that undertakes longhaul cargo flights to Asia, the Pacific Rim, Africa, the Middle East and North America using eight 747-200/400 Freighters (Cargolux was the first operator of the 747-400 Freighter, and has accelerated delivery of its fourth from September 1998 to August 1997).

Cargo Lion is a charter cargo airline with a small number of DC-8-62 Freighters.

Macedonia

With one airport for scheduled flights, this small republic has two airlines operating from the capital Skopje, namely Macedonian Airlines with a 737-200 and Palair Macedonian Airlines. The latter is an IATA member, with two Fokker 100s, two F28s and a BAC One-Eleven for its services to 13 or more European destinations.

Macau

As the only airline of Macau (which is situated on the southern coast of China), the recently founded Air Macau has two A320s and two A321s for its flights into China and other regional destinations in Asia.

Madagascar

The Republic of Madagascar, off the east coast of Africa, has a population of about 15 million served by 18 airports handling scheduled flights. The flag airline is Air Madagascar, an IATA member, founded in 1962 and operating out of the capital Antananarivo. With three 737s, a 747 Combi, two BAe 748s and several Twin Otters, it flies a busy domestic network and makes international connections to the Comoros Islands, Djibouti, France, Kenya, Mauritius, Réunion Island, South Africa and Switzerland.

Transport et Travaux Aériens de Madagascar serves domestic and regional points in concert with Air Madagascar operations, using two ATR 42s.

TOP
A Lithuanian Airlines Boeing 737-200

ABOVE
One of Cargolux's Boeing 747-400 Freighters

OPPOSITE,
ABOVE
One of Air Madagascar's three 737s, a series 300

BELOW
Malaysia Airlines has 12 Boeing 747-400s in its operational fleet of some 90 aircraft

Malawi

Malawi has six airports. Air Malawi is the state-owned national airline (IATA member), operating to a small number of domestic points from Blantyre and regionally to Kenya, Mozambique, South Africa, Tanzania, Zambia and Zimbabwe using a 737-300, ATR 42 and a Dornier 228.

Malaysia

Of six Malaysian airlines, all but one are scheduled domestic or domestic/regional operators with typically small/medium turboprop airliners, although Transmile Air Services' 13 or so aircraft include a larger 737 pure jet.

Malaysia Airlines, founded in 1937, is the main international airline, also retaining regional and domestic routes. Beginning life as Malayan Airways Ltd., and formed by the Ocean Steamship Company of Liverpool and the Straits Steamship Company of Singapore, it did not inaugurate services until 1947.

It became a public limited company in 1958 and in 1966 the governments of Malaysia and Singapore acquired majority control, adopting the new name Malaysia-Singapore Airlines in 1967. The governmental partnership was dissolved in 1971 and the airline then became Malaysia's national carrier as Malaysia Airline System. The present name was adopted in 1987.

In mid-1996 Malaysia Airlines owned 96 aircraft, with 28 on order (the latter including 15 777-200/-300s and ten 747-400s for delivery from 1997). Of the current fleet, four DC-10s, A300s, five 737-400s and two Fokker 50s were leased out, while two MD-11s, an MD-11 Freighter, an A330 and Fokker 50 were leased in, giving the airline an in-system fleet of some 90 aircraft (12 747-400s, one 747-300, two 747-200s, two MD-11s, one MD-11F, 11 A330s, an A300, 34 737-400s, nine 737-500s, two 737-300Fs, nine Fokker 50s and six Twin Otters).

According to figures for the latest available

yearly period, 13,093,000 passengers were carried over an accumulated 21,003,448,000 RPK, producing a passenger load factor of 69.8 per cent. In addition to this, cargo accounted for 913,176,000 tonne-kilometres, not including mail. Thirty-six domestic destinations were served in July 1996, as well as 78 international, the latter as four in the Americas, nine in Europe plus six more through code sharing, eight in the south-west Pacific plus four code shared, 13 in north Asia, 19 in south-east Asia, and ten in west Asia/Africa plus one code shared and four as joint services.

Malaysia Airlines
Address: 33rd Floor, Bangunan MAS,
Jalan Sultan Ismail, 50250 Kuala Lumpur,
Malaysia (GPO Box 10513, 50716).
Telephone: +60 3 2610555
Fax: +60 3 2613472

Maldives

This Indian Ocean island group has a single airport for scheduled flights. The national carrier is Air Maldives, which operates a tiny fleet on scheduled/charter services from the capital Male to four domestic points and a small number of international destinations.

Malta

Air Malta was founded by a Resolution of Malta's House of Representatives on 21 March 1973, with the aim of establishing, maintaining, developing and operating passenger, cargo and mail air transport services to serve the national interest. Operations began on 1 April 1974 with two wet-leased Boeing 720Bs. Today, the airline serves 48 destinations in Europe, North Africa and the Middle East, plus some 20 charter points in the UK and a similar number in mainland Europe. Subsidiaries include Malta Air Charter, a helicopter airlink and sightseeing company.

The latest available yearly figures showed that Air Malta carried 1.36 million passengers (scheduled and charter), a growth of 7.5 per cent over the previous year. RPK totalled over 1,652 million. The current fleet comprises two A320-200s, one wet-leased A310-200, two 737-200Advs, five 737-300s (one dry-leased) and four RJ70s.

Air Malta
Address: Luqa LQA 01, Malta.
Telephone: +356 690890-9
Fax: +356 673241

A small charter airline, with mainly C-212s, is Mediterranean Aviation.

Mariana Islands

Pacific Island Aviation has three Bandeirantes and seven Cessnas for commuter and cargo services linking Saipan with neighbouring Tinian, Guam and Rota.

Marshall Islands

The government-owned Air Marshall Islands has a DC-8-62F plus various turboprop airliners (including Saab 2000s and Dornier 228s) for its extensive passenger and cargo network.

Mauritius

Air Mauritius, the national carrier, was established on 14 June 1967 and started operations as a handling company in 1968. From a leased Piper Navajo in 1972, it now has three A340-300s (two more for 1998-99 delivery), two 767-200ERs, one leased 767-300ER, two ATR 42s (two more for 1997 delivery), and two Bell JetRanger helicopters.

Figures indicate that 679,000 passengers were carried in 1996, allowing an RPK total of 3,215 million. In addition, 18,214 tons (18,707 tonnes) of cargo also transported. The network of 25 destinations encompasses points in Europe, Asia, Africa and Australia, including the Rodrigues Island and Réunion in the Indian Ocean (*see* British Airways).

Air Mauritius
Address: Air Mauritius Centre,
President John Kennedy Street, PO Box 441, Port Louis, Mauritius.
Telephone: +230 2087700
Fax: +230 2088331

Mexico

Of twenty or more Mexican airlines, four are members of IATA, namely Aérovias de Mexico (AeroMexico), its subsidiary Aeromexpress, Mexicana, and Transportes Aéreos Ejecutivos (TAESA). Interestingly, Aeromexpress (founded on 1 December 1989) is a cargo airline serving 45 domestic destinations plus 16 in the USA, three in Central America, 21 in South America, one in Canada and two in Europe. With two 727-200 freighters of its own, by belonging to the CINTRA Corporation (AeroMexico Group) it also has the back-up of AeroMexico, Mexicana, Aerolitoral, AeroPerú and Aerocaribe.

Aeromexpress
Address: Av. Texcoco s/n, esq. Av. Tahel,
Col Peñón de los Baños 15620, Mexico D.F.
Telephone: +52 237 02 03
Fax: +52 237 02 26

Founded in 1934, Aérovias de Mexico (AeroMexico) is a national airline offering both domestic and international services. It was restructured in 1995 to reduce APK capacity by 13 per cent, to 14,254 million, by the return of three leased DC-10s and two MD-82s. Its current fleet thereby comprises 51 aircraft, as two 767-300s, six 757-200s, 25 MD-80s and 18 DC-9s. Employment level then stood at an average 5,355 persons.

During the latest full year, AeroMexico carried 6,791,000 passengers, accumulating 8,519 million RPK. In addition to its subsidiary, Aeromexpress, it owns 47 per cent of the shares in AeroPerú, a 99 per cent equity holding in Servicios Aéreos Litoral (Aerolitoral), and a 45.9 per cent holding in Mexicana.

Aérovias de Mexico (AeroMexico)
Address: Paseo de la Reforma No 445,
C.P. 06500, Mexico D.F.
Telephone: +52 5 327 4000
Fax: +52 5 625 2621

Mexicana itself flies to 32 domestic destinations plus 17 international cities in the USA (eight), Canada (Montreal), Central America (three), South America (four) and Cuba, with a fleet that in June 1996 comprised ten Fokker 100s, 12 A320s and 22 727s. Eight further A320s were on order in June 1996. Subsidiaries include Aerocaribe (two DC-9s plus Fairchild F-27 types).

Mexicana's origins can be traced to Compañia Mexicana De Transportación Aérea, founded on 12 July 1921 and initially specializing in payroll deliveries. During the 1930s it became Mexico's foremost airline and in 1935 began a scheduled service between Mexico City and Los Angeles, the first foreign airline to receive such US approval. Jet services were inaugurated in 1960, using de Havilland Comet 4Cs.

Mexicana
Address: Xola 535 Piso 17,
Col. Del Valle, 03100 Mexico D.F.
Telephone: +52 5 227 02 60
Fax: +52 5 523 23 64

Privately-owned Transportes Aéreos Ejecutivos (TAESA) has four divisions, namely corporate aviation, charter, cargo and scheduled. It was founded on 27 April 1988 as an air taxi operator, with a cargo division following in 1989 (equipped with two 727-100s) while domestic charter services began in 1990 (international flights added later), joined from 12 February 1991 by the opening of the scheduled division. The present commercial fleet comprises three 737-200As, six 737-300s, three 737-500s, three 727-100 freighters, four 727-100 Combis, two 727-200s, two 757-200s, five DC-9-15s, one DC-10-30F freighter, and one DC-10-30.

With an amazing growth rate (122 per cent in 1993), TAESA holds 27 per cent of Mexico's domestic market and flies one of the country's largest fleets. The scheduled division covers 21 points in Mexico and four in the USA. The charter division covers 76 cities in Canada, the USA, Europe, the Caribbean, Central and South America and Japan, flying up to 600,000 passengers annually, mainly to Mexico's tourist destinations. Cargo destinations total 20. The airline as a whole has some 3,500 employees, including 300 pilots, and the daily unduplicated route network totals on average 75,800 miles (122,000 km) for scheduled, 30,450 miles

(49,000 km) for charter and 8,075 miles (13,000 km) for cargo flights. A parcels service was launched in 1995 as TAESAExpress.

Transportes Aéreos Ejecutivos (TAESA)
Address: PO Box 9-212, Mexico City International Airport, Mexico City 15001, Mexico.
Telephone: +52 5 227 0727
Fax: +52 5 227 4044

Moldova

The Republic of Moldova has one airport for scheduled flights. The flag airline is Air Moldova, with a fleet of more than 30 aircraft to operate over a network of 15 European destinations. Aircraft include eight Tu-154Bs, ten Tu-134s and Antonov An-24/26/32s.

Moldavian Airlines flies to seven European points using four Yak-40/42s.

Mongolia

MIAT Mongolian Airlines has a broad spectrum of activities. These include domestic and a small number of international flights from its hub at the nation's single airport for scheduled services at the capital Ulaanbaatar, agricultural work and air ambulance duties. Its fleet is headed by some 12 An-24s, with other aircraft including further Antonovs, five Y-12s, three 727s, and Mi-8 helicopters.

Montenegro

Operating out of Podgorica, Air Montenegro began flying again in 1996 after a United Nation's ban on air activities was lifted. Using an all-leased fleet comprising a BAe 146, 737-200 and two Yaks, it offers charter flights to Albania, Italy, Turkey and Yugoslavia.

Morocco

Royal Air Maroc, as the national airline, is mostly Government owned, though both Air France and Iberia have small share interests. Founded in 1953, it operates out of Casablanca to domestic points plus 19 destinations in the Middle East and Africa,

28 cities in Europe, and single points in Brazil, the USA and Canada.

The fleet is entirely Boeing based, with the exception of two ATR 42 turboprop airliners, and includes two 757-200s, two 747s, 19 737-200/400/500s, and the last remaining 727s. Nine 737-800s are on order for delivery from 1998.

Royal Air Maroc
Address: Aéroport ANFA Casablanca, Morocco.
Telephone: +212 2 912000
Fax: +212 2 912093, 912054

Mozambique

With eight airports handling scheduled flights, this large African nation has Linhas Aéreas de Moçambique as its Government-owned national airline. Originating in 1936, it operates from the capital Maputo to take in six domestic points plus international services to South Africa, Zimbabwe and Portugal. In addition to four small C-212s, it has a TriStar and two 737s for passenger and cargo carrying.

Myanmar

Formerly known as Burma, this nation has no fewer than 19 airports for scheduled flights. Myanmar

Airways is the state airline, originally known as Union of Burma Airways when founded in 1948. From its hub at Yangon (Rangoon), it flies over a regional network of more than 20 destinations using a single 757-200, one 737-400, three F28s and several F27s.

TOP
One of AeroMexico's two Boeing 767-300s

CENTRE
One of 12 Mexicana Airbus A320s

ABOVE
TAESA Boeing 757 and 737

OPPOSITE
Air Malta Airbus A320-200

47

Namibia

Air Namibia is a division of TransNamib Ltd. which is also engaged in rail, road and sea transportation in Namibia. The airline has had four different names over the past 40 years, taking its present title after the nation's declaration of independence in 1990 when it became the national airline. It currently employs 335 people.

In July 1996, of using Windhoek International Airport as its main hub, the airline flew international services to and from London and Frankfurt using a 747SP. Regional services are to eight points in Zambia, Zimbabwe, Botswana, Angola and South Africa, and domestic flights are to 11 cities, the regional and domestic operations undertaken by one 737-200A, a Dash 8 and three Beech 1900s. One of the Beech 1900s is available for charter.

Air Namibia
Address: PO Box 731, Windhoek 9000, Namibia.
Telephone: +264 61 223019
Fax: +264 61 221910

Nauru

Air Nauru is the republic's national airline, operating five 737s to 10 destinations on other Pacific islands, in the Philippines and Australia.

Nepal

Everest Air, Necon Air and Nepal Airways are regional and/or domestic airlines flying turboprop aircraft (mainly BAe 748s, Dornier 228s and Harbin Y-12s). The national airline is Royal Nepal Airlines, founded in 1958 and operating domestic services plus routes to France, Germany, Hong Kong, India, Singapore, Thailand and the UK with a mixed fleet of pure jets and turboprop aircraft that in June 1996 included two 757-200s.

Netherlands

Founded on 7 October 1919, KLM Royal Dutch Airlines' first-ever scheduled commercial flight took off from London bound for Amsterdam on 17 May 1920. Services on this route are the oldest still operated by the original airline flying under the same name. Early flights used wet-leased aircraft from the British airline AT&T, but these services were suspended on 31 October that year because of the open accommodation for passengers, to be restarted on 14 April 1921 using the airline's own enclosed-cabin Fokker F2s and F3s. KLM's first turbine aircraft, a turboprop Vickers Viscount, was acquired in 1957 and it became the first European airline to order the DC-8 pure-jet, arriving in 1960.

For the year up to 31 March 1996, KLM recorded a total RPK of 45,531 million, the largest percentage from North American services and attaining a passenger load factor of 74.4 per cent. Revenue ton-kilometre for cargo was 3,813 million. The consolidated KLM fleet, when including its subsidiary KLM Cityhopper, comprises five 747-400s (including 4 financial leases), 11 747-400Ms (financial leases), three 747-300s (financial leases), ten 747-300Ms (including five financial leases), nine MD-11s (including eight financial leases), five A310-200s (including 2 financial leases), 12 737-400s (financial leases), 29 737-300s (including eight financial and ten operational leases), one 737-200, three 767-300ERs (operational leases), four 757s (three financial and one operational leases), six Fokker 100s (financial leases), two Fokker 70s

(operational leases), ten Fokker 50s (financial leases), four F28s and 11 Saab 340Bs (including ten financial leases). A 767-300ER for KLM was historically the 8,000th commercial jetliner delivered by Boeing, on 1 March 1996.

KLM Royal Dutch Airlines
Address: Amsterdamseweg 55,
1182 GP Amstelveen, Netherlands.
Telephone: +31 20 649 9123
Fax: +31 20 648 8092

Of the other Dutch airlines, only Transavia Airlines is a member of IATA, operating a large fleet of 757-200s and 737-300s on international and regional scheduled flights. It ordered eight 737-800s in November 1995, with options for 12 more, for delivery from 1997.

Netherlands Antilles
This island grouping off Venezuela has ALM Antillean Airlines and Windward Island Airways International flying regional services, the former, an IATA member, using three MD-82s and two Dash 8s.

New Caledonia
IATA member Air Caledonie International was founded in September 1983, undertaking its first services on 3 December that year over the Melbourne/Nouméa/Melbourne connections using a 747 in association with Qantas. The current fleet comprises a 737-300 and a Twin Otter, used on routes to Vila, Wallis, Nandi, Sydney, Brisbane, Melbourne, Auckland, Papeete, and Wallis-Futuna (Twin Otter). The total number of passengers carried in the latest full year was 116,046, and 178 staff were then employed.

Air Caledonie International
Address: 8 rue Frédéric Surleau, BP 3736,
Nouméa, Nouvelle-Calédonie
Telephone: +687 26 55 46
Fax: +687 27 27 72

The domestic operator is Air Calédonie, connecting Île des Pins, Maré, Tiga, Lifu, Ouvéa, Nouméa, Koné, Touho, Koumac, Poum and Belep using three ATR 42s among other aircraft.

New Zealand
Four of New Zealand's airlines are IATA members, namely Air New Zealand, Ansett New Zealand, Mount Cook Group and Pacific Midland Airlines.

Air New Zealand has its origins in Tasman Empire Airways Limited (TEAL) which was founded on 26 April 1940 by the New Zealand Government, Union Airways, BOAC and Qantas, beginning services between Auckland and Sydney on 30 April with a Short S.30 Empire flying-boat. Other flying-boats followed into service, though in 1948 DC-4 landplanes chartered from TAA were used to maintain schedules when Tasman-class flying-boats were temporarily grounded. TEAL became fully New

Zealand-owned in 1961 and in 1965 took its present name. A domestic carrier established in 1947 as New Zealand National Airways Corporation (NAC) merged with Air New Zealand in 1978 and privatization followed in 1988.

With its main base/hub in Auckland and hubs in Los Angeles, Honolulu and Brisbane, Air New Zealand has a passenger and cargo network covering 35 airports in 19 countries. Domestic main trunk jet services are supplemented by provincial services operated by subsidiary airlines under the New Zealand Link banner, namely Air New Zealand National (12 737-200Advs); Mount Cook Group (fleet includes seven ATR 72s); Air Nelson (eight Fairchild Metroliners and 12 Saab 340As); and Eagle Air (four Metroliners and nine Bandeirantes).

The main Air New Zealand fleet comprises four 747-400s, five 747-200s, seven 767-300ERs and five 767-200ERs. The airline also provides handling services to many of the international carriers operating into the country, plus pilot training, and undertakes a wide range of engineering work. Over the latest full year, the airline carried 2,756,000 passengers on international flights and 3,626,000 on domestic routes, accumulating 16,086 million and 1,637 million RPK respectively.

Air New Zealand
Address: Quay Tower, 29 Customs Street West,
Private Bag 92007, Auckland 1, New Zealand.
Telephone: +64 9 366 2400
Fax: +64 9 366 2759

Ansett New Zealand began its scheduled domestic services in July 1987, after amendment of the Air Services Act permitted foreign investment in a domestic airline. It currently carries 1.9 million passengers a year, achieving an average load factor of 71.1 per cent. More than 1,150 staff are employed, including 142 pilots.

ABOVE
Air Caledonie International Boeing 737-300 in new livery

OPPOSITE, ABOVE
Air Namibia Boeing 747SP and 737-200A
(Keith Woosey)

BELOW
KLM Boeing 747-400 operating longhaul flights from Amsterdam's Schiphol Airport

The Ansett New Zealand fleet comprises eight BAe 146-300s and a BAe 146-200 QC (quick convertible, for passengers by day and freight at night), occupied over its main trunk routes linking Auckland, Wellington, Christchurch and Dunedin and also for the tourist route of Rotorua, Christchurch and Queenstown, while four Dash 8s link seven points. The airline's commuter service, Ansett New Zealand Regional, operates four Bandeirantes.

Ansett New Zealand
Address: 50 Grafton Road, PO Box 4168,
Auckland, New Zealand.
Telephone: +64 9 309 6235
Fax: +64 9 309 6434

Nicaragua

Nicaraguenses de Aviación (Nica) has the airport at the capital Managua as its main base, one of four airports handling scheduled flights in the country. Founded in 1992 as the nation's flag airline, it has one 737-200 and a C-212 for its regional and domestic operations.

Nigeria

Of seventeen or more Nigerian airlines, only the national carrier, Nigeria Airways, is an IATA member. Founded in June 1958 from the previous West African Airways that had itself been established only two years earlier (in May 1956), it flies to 19 domestic points plus various regional destinations in Africa and internationally to Jeddah, New York,

Amsterdam, London and Rome. Its fleet is headed by four A310s and five 737-200s, with other aircraft including a DC-10-30.

Of the other non-IATA Nigerian airlines, of particular interest is Okada Air, which is among the largest privately-owned airlines of the continent. It has a fleet of about 20 BAC One-Elevens plus a 747, three 727s and a 707 for its domestic and international, scheduled and charter, passenger and cargo operations.

Norway

The two Norwegian IATA airlines are very different, with Braathens S.A.F.E. flying a large pure-jet fleet over international and domestic routes, while Widerøe's Flyveselskap is a domestic airline with turboprop aircraft. Not to be overlooked, however, is Norwegian Airlines (DNL, Det Norske Luftselskap), forming part of the SAS consortium (*see* Sweden), itself an IATA member.

Celebrating 50 years of flying in 1996, Braathens S.A.F.E. was founded on 26 March 1946 and began operations with three DC-4s. It was intended to supplement the Braathens merchant ship fleet and is today still run by the same family. The first flights were to South America and the Far East, hence the initials S.A.F.E., which came to form part of the name.

Braathens S.A.F.E is Norway's largest airline, carrying 4.5 million passengers yearly from its base in Oslo to 14 domestic destinations ranging from Kristiansand in the south to Longyearbyen in the north, a passenger figure which rises to nearly 5 million when added to the number carried to nine foreign destinations plus charter flights. It is also the largest carrier of air freight in Norway. The present fleet comprises 18 737-500s and seven 737-400s. Employees total 3,160.

Braathens S.A.F.E.
Address: Oksenøyveien 3, PO Box 55,
1330 Oslo Lufthavn, Norway.
Telephone: +47 67 59 70 00
Fax: +47 67 53 96 46

The other IATA airline is Widerøe's Flyveselskap, established on 19 February 1934 and today the third largest Norwegian airline. Its primary function is in serving the STOL (short take-off and landing) network in Norway, plus commercial services and charter/wet-lease operations. It also owns Widerøe Norsk Air, which was merging in 1996, based on a uniform fleet of Dash 8s.

A total of 1,126,504 passengers flew with Widerøe in the last full year, with Widerøe's Flyveselskap accounting for 969,134 passengers (recording 191.738 million passenger-kilometres) plus 5,568 tons (5,657 tonnes) of mail and freight on its STOL network. The fleet then comprised (in 1995) 15 Dash 8 series 103s, one Dash 8 series 300, one Twin Otter and three Dash 7s.

Pakistan

The Pakistan International Airlines' network now spans 36 domestic cities plus 52 international destinations in 46 countries of four continents. PIA was founded in 1954 and is the flag airline of Pakistan. Historically, its first regular service was inaugurated on 10 May 1954 using a Super Constellation. In 1959 it introduced a leased 707-320 onto its London route to become the first Asian airline to fly a pure jet, and in 1963 was the first non-communist airline to fly into China.

TOP
A Nigerian regional airline is Afrimex Aviation which ordered three Dornier 328s and placed options for nine more

CENTRE
Braathens S.A.F.E. has an all-Boeing 737 fleet

ABOVE
One of two Lapsa – Air Paraguay Airbus airliners

OPPOSITE,
TOP
An Air New Zealand Boeing 767-300 in latest livery

OPPOSITE,
BELOW
Ansett New Zealand BAe 146-300

Employing a yearly average of 20,688 persons, including 560 captains/co-pilots/cadet pilots, the PIA fleet of 46 aircraft comprises eight 747-200s, nine A300B4s, six A310-300s, six 737-200s, two 707 freighters, 13 F27s and two Twin Otters. In the latest full year it carried 5,517,000 revenue passengers, accumulating over 10,382 million RPK.

Pakistan International Airlines
Address: Quaid-e-Azam International Airport, Karachi 75200, Pakistan.
Telephone: +92 21 4572011
Fax: +92 21 7727727

Panama
Compañia Panameña de Aviación (Copa), as Panama's principal airline, was founded in 1947 by Panamanian businessmen, who obtained the technical assistance and equity participation of Pan American Airways (Pan Am's equity was sold to Panamanian investors in the 1970s). Starting with three ex-military C-47s (DC-3s) for domestic flights, it was not until the mid-1960s that international operations began, initially to Costa Rica.

Expansion of services has been continuous, and in 1996 further South American routes were planned in addition to the 21 current destinations in Panama and to Colombia, Costa Rica, the Dominican Republic, Honduras, Jamaica, Nicaragua, Puerto Rico and the USA. Cargo and passenger charters are also offered. In the last full year, 661,185 passengers and 26,493,000 lb (12,017,000 kg) of cargo were carried over an accumulated 861 million RPK, and for 1997 the anticipated passenger total is expected to rise to about 725,000.

Compañia Panameña de Aviación
Address: Avenida Justo Arosemena y Calle 39, Apartado 1572 Panamá 1, Panamá.
Telephone: +507 227 0116, 0233, 4551
Fax: +507 227 1952

Other Panamanian airlines include AeroPerlas and Alas Chiricanas, operating turboprop aircraft. The latest airline is Trans Canal Airways, intended initially for flights to Miami with Fokker 70s and BAe 146s.

Papua New Guinea
Air Niugini is the largest of the Melanesian and Polynesian airlines operating in the South Pacific. It has a route network, from its base at Port Moresby, serving 20 provincial points in Papua New Guinea plus eight in neighbouring Indonesia, the Solomon Islands and Australia, and destinations in Asia, Singapore, Manila and Hong Kong.

Air Niugini inaugurated services on 1 November 1973 to Lae, Rabaul and Kieta. Today, it has a fleet of two A310-300s, six F28-1000, one F28-4000 and two Dash 7s (the latter partly for freight operations). In joint services with Philippine Airlines, Qantas and Singapore Airlines, it also offers 767 flights. The latest full year figures show that the airline carried 174,233 passengers on international and 687,887 on domestic flights.

Air Niugini
Address: PO Box 7186, Boroko, Papua New Guinea.
Telephone: +675 327 3200
Fax: +675 327 3482

Paraguay
Lapsa – Air Paraguay is the national airline, established through privatization of the former state-owned Líneas Aéreas Paraguayas in October 1994, after which only a 20 per cent stake remained in

Government hands. Lapsa's inaugural flight took place in February 1995, to Buenos Aires.

Currently with some 250 employees, it has a fleet of two 737-200s, one A320-232 and one A310-304 with which to operate from Asunción to Buenos Aires, Montevideo, Santiago, São Paulo, Santa Cruz, Lima, Quito, Guayaquil, Miami, Ciudad del Este, Aruba and Punta Cana. In the latest full operating year it carried 105,154 passengers plus 1,789 tons (1,818 tonnes) of cargo.

Lapsa – Air Paraguay
Address: Peru 456, Asunción, Paraguay.
Telephone: +595 21 491 040
Fax: +595 21 496 484

Peru

There are seven principal airlines in Peru. AeroPerú (Empresa de Transporte Aéreo del Perú) is the only IATA member and has AeroMexico as a major shareholder. Founded in the early 1970s as a Government-owned airline born out of previously-operated military services, though privatized in 1981, it flies a domestic network and also connects foreign destinations in the Americas from its main hub at Lima, using a fleet of two 757-200s, six 727s and an F28.

Compañia de Aviación Faucett has a mainly domestic network of scheduled and charter services with a larger mixed fleet that includes several 737s, but also undertakes international flights to Miami and elsewhere. It was founded in 1928 by the American barnstorming aviator, Elmer Faucett.

Americana uses 727s for scheduled services, while the only airline with Russian-supplied equipment is Imperial Air (An-32s and Tu-134As). Aero Continente and Aero Santa offer charter flights with 727s and 737s, and Aeronaves del Perú has 707 and DC-8 freighters for charter.

Philippines

Philippine Airlines was founded on 25 February 1941 following the collapse of Philippine Air Transport. It began limited services on 15 March with Beech aircraft. However, operations were halted that December following the Japanese invasion. Using ex-military C-47s, flights resumed on 14 February 1946.

Recent operating losses have forced reappraisal of its current route network and aircraft, and the airline is now becoming heavily dependent on Airbus airliners. In September 1996 the airline operated 12 A300s and a A340, and had 12 A320s, eight A330s and seven A340s on order, while the rest of its then current fleet comprised 12 747-200/400s (a 747-400 Combi and seven 747-400s are on order), a similar number of 737-300s, two

DC-10-30s and ten Fokker 50s.

Another Philippine Airbus operator is Grand International Airways with three A300s, while Pacific East Asia Cargo Airlines has four BAe 146QT, 737 and 727 freighters for domestic /regional cargo/package deliveries (TNT is a shareholder).

Poland

LOT Polish Airlines is the national carrier, founded on 1 January 1929. It joined IATA in 1931 and became a joint stock company of the State Treasury in 1992. Recent accolades have included a Business Travel World '96 award for the 'Best Business Airline in Eastern Europe'.

Having recently withdrawn the last of its Russian-built airliners, LOT now has a fleet comprising eight ATR 72s, six 737-500s, five 737-400s, two 767-200ERs and two 767-300ERs, while a further 767-300ER will be received in 1997 and two 737-800s (ordered in October 1996) will be delivered in 1998. The average age of its aircraft was just 3.9 years in June 1996.

Based at Warsaw Okecie International Airport and with 107 offices worldwide, the airline's route network serves six domestic points and 47 foreign destinations in Europe (34), Africa, the Middle East, Far East and North America. In the latest full year it carried 1,839,367 passengers, accumulating

43,289,400 passenger-kilometres. Employees then totalled 3,982. Subsidiaries include Air Tours Poland.

LOT Polish Airlines
Address: 39, 17 Stycznia Street, 00-906 Warsaw, Poland.
Telephone: +48 22 606 61 11
Fax: +48 22 46 09 09

Portugal

TAP Air Portugal has its origins in Transportes Aéreos Portugueses, created on 14 March 1945. Using DC-3s, commercial operations began on 19 September 1946, between Lisbon and Madrid, while in 1953 the airline became a private company, though the State still held most shares. On 2 August 1962 a Caravelle service to Madrid opened its jet era and in 1975 it was nationalized as a public company.

TAP's current fleet comprises four A340-300s, six A320-200s, five A310-300s, eight 737-300s, eight 737-200s and any remaining TriStar 500s (of five, put up for sale). In the latest full year, 3,696,376 passengers were carried as well as huge quantities of cargo plus mail over a combined distance of 46,593,350 miles (74,984,752 km). The number of employees stood at 8,217. Its route network reaches 52 domestic and international destinations, mainly within Europe, and to the Americas and Africa but also including Tel Aviv and a new 1996 service to Macau.

TAP Air Portugal
Address: Apartado 50194, 1704 Lisboa Codex, Lisbon, Portugal.
Telephone: +351 1 841 5000
Fax: +351 1 841 5095

Portugalia has six Fokker 100s for scheduled and charter flights, and SATA Air Acores is a charter airline with a 737-300 and four turboprop aircraft.

Qatar

With only one airport for scheduled flights in the country, Qatar Airways uses the capital Doha as its base. Founded in 1993, it flies to Abu Dhabi, Dubai, Egypt, India, Japan, Kuwait, Muscat, Taiwan, Thailand, UK (London), and the UAE, using a fleet of three 747s and three 727s. A helicopter charter company is Gulf Helicopters.

Réunion

This small island in the Indian Ocean has one airport for scheduled flights at Saint-Denis, the capital city, from where Air Austral operates its 737-500 and 737-300 on scheduled services that link seven regional destinations.

Romania

Of several Romanian airlines, the State has major interests in Tarom (Transporturile Aeriene Romane – Romanian Air Transport) and Romavia Romanian Aviation. The latter was founded in 1991 and flies scheduled and charter services using a mixed fleet of Russian-supplied and Western airliners, freighters and helicopters, including three 1-11 types, four Antonov An-24/26s and a 707. The main private sector airline is Jaro International, which inaugurated charter services in 1991 and has two 1-11 types, four 707s and other aircraft.

Tarom was founded in 1954, after Soviet interests in the 1946-established Transporturile Aeriene Romana Sovietica (TARS) were bought out.

Operating from Bucharest, it connects 33 European cities, nine in the Middle East, two in the USA plus China, India and Thailand. Its fleet is headed by two A310s (a third has been ordered), joined by five Tu-154s, 12 1-11 types, five 737-300s, over 20 An-24/26s, and Il-18/707 freighters.

Russia

The partition of the former Soviet Union into separate republics, and the drive towards a more commercially free society, led to a huge and almost uncontrollable rise in the number of airlines registered within the CIS, and in particular in Russia. By the start of 1996, more than 460 airlines were registered in Russia alone, but due to stringent checks some 76 were forced to temporarily or permanently cease operations, while nearly 20 more will not have their licences renewed. Of the remainder there are about 170 significant airlines, of which about one-third each have ten or more medium/large aircraft, while the great bulk of all passengers and cargoes are carried by a mere 17 airlines, only two of which are IATA members.

Once the world's largest airline, Aeroflot has seen many of its former regional divisions hived off to form the national carriers of the independent CIS republics or become separate privatized airlines, a good example of the former being ORBI Georgian Airlines (see Georgia). The current Aeroflot – Russian International Airlines is owned by the Russian State (51 per cent) and some 15,000 employees. It is the official Russian international flag airline, with a network encompassing destinations in nine CIS republics and over 100 other countries worldwide, though its domestic services only span half a dozen cities.

The original Aeroflot was founded in 1932 out of Dobroflot, the State airline established in 1929 and itself born out of Dobrolet of 1923 inauguration. In addition to passenger and cargo carrying, Aeroflot was obliged to undertake other air activities on behalf of the State, including agricultural spraying and surveying.

Today's Aeroflot remains committed to flying mainly Russian aircraft plus two huge Ukrainian Antonov freighters. It has been taking in new Tu-204s while simultaneously improving its Ilyushins by refurbishing the older wide-body Il-86s and fitting new engines to Il-76s. But Western aircraft are beginning to make some impact on the fleet and in addition to eight A310s (three leased), two leased 767-300ERs were taken into service in 1994, their flight crews and technicians trained in Seattle. The rest of the Aeroflot fleet comprises 25 Tu-154Ms, five older Tu-154s and 13 Tu-134s, about four Tu-204Cs, six Il-96-300s, well over 20 Il-62Ms, 18 Il-86s, up to 18 Il-76 freighters, two An-124-100s and a DC-10F freighter. Aircraft on order include ten westernized Il-96M passenger airliners and ten westernized Il-96T freighters.

Aeroflot – Russian International Airlines
Address: 37 Leningradsky Prospekt,
125157 Moscow, Russian Federation.
Telephone: +7 095 155 6641, 6534
Fax: +7 095 155 6647

The other Russian IATA airline is Transaero Airlines, a joint stock company that has Transaero Express as a subsidiary (90 per cent shareholding). It was incorporated on 28 December 1990 under the Law of Enterprise and Business in Russia and in accordance with the Joint-Stock Companies Regulations ratified

on 21 December 1990, starting its own operations on 5 November 1991. It became the first Russian airline to take in a new Boeing airliner (757 in 1994, to complement the two 737-200s then already operated), and was re-registered on 18 August 1994.

With 2,209 employees, of which 189 are flight crew, Transaero has a network of 26 CIS and international destinations, including London and Paris flown via Riga on a code-share basis with Riga Airlines (see Riair, Latvia). However, a direct route to London is among eight planned new scheduled services for 1996-97, which also include Chicago (USA), T'aipei (Taiwan) and Cairo (Egypt). The airline also operates charter services to over 20 destinations. In the latest full year, 1,182,000 passengers were carried, offering an RPK of 3,058 million from an available seat-kilometre total of 4,175 millon. The fleet comprises one owned Il-86 plus five 737s, five 757s and three DC-10-30s, the Western aircraft all leased.

Transaero Airlines
Address: GosNIIGA, Building 3,
Sheremetyevo Airport, 103340 Moscow,
Russian Federation.
Telephone: +7 095 5785060, 5785038
Fax: +7 095 5788688

Of the many other Russian airlines, space permits mention of only a few. Aerovolga has a mixed Russian/Ukrainian fleet that includes 11 Tu-154s for its regional domestic services from Samara, while a major State-run international and domestic passenger/cargo airline with nine Il-86s and well over 20 Tu-154B/Ms among its fleet is Aviation Enterprise Pulkovo.

AVL – Arkhangelskie operates regional/domestic services out of Arkhangelsk with about 32 aircraft that include Il-114s received since March 1995. Bikovo Avialinii (a division of Aeroflot) flies a very extensive regional network from Bykovo airport in Moscow, while detachments based in the Moscow Region have their own large fleets.

KrasAir is a private joint-stock company based in Krasnoyarsk, Siberia. It was a division of Aeroflot until 1993. Its large number of mainly Russian and Ukrainian airliners, freighters and helicopters has been joined by DC-10-30 freighters. Myachkovo, operating out of the Moscow Region airport of that name, is interesting for having many An-30

survey/photogrammetry aircraft and An-2s (plus helicopters), indicating its primary survey and mapping services that are now supplemented by passenger/cargo charters.

Among newer Russian airliners is the Tu-204, which formed the basis of a freighter conversion taken into service alongside passenger models by Oriol-Avia Airlines. The very first airline to receive the Tu-204 had been, however, Vnukovo Airlines in Moscow in 1993. Vnukovo was founded that same year as a large privatized division of Aeroflot, its fleet also including 22 Il-86s and a generally similar number of Tu-154 variants.

Other operators of Tu-204s include Rossiya Airlines, a charter airline with over 50 passenger and cargo aircraft that encompass Il-96s and two or more examples of the world's largest production freighter, the An-124. Rossiya is the Russian Government Air Services unit of Aeroflot. Other An-124 operators include the Aeroflot subsidiary AJAX and VolgaDnepr based at Ulyanovsk for worldwide freighting. HeavyLift in the UK and VolgaDnepr co-operate over freighting services.

Diamond Sakha Airlines based in Nerungri has two leased A310-200s among its otherwise Russian/Ukrainian fleet for international and domestic services, while companion Diamond Russia Sakha is a charter cargo operator.

The Moscow-based Samara Airlines flies to more than 60 Russian/CIS destinations and also offers international routes to Austria, India, Israel, Turkey and elsewhere using some 30 aircraft, while Siberia Airlines at Novosibirsk has Il-86s within its large fleet for international and domestic

ABOVE
Aeroflot – Russian International Airlines leases two Boeing 767-300ERs

OPPOSITE, ABOVE
TAP Air Portugal Airbus A340-300

INSET
Baikal Airlines based in the central Siberian city of Irkutsk has a leased Boeing 757-200 among well over 50 airliners, plus helicopters

OPPOSITE, BELOW
DAC AIR, Romanian Regional Airlines, is to receive four Bombardier Canadair Regional Jets (as shown). It has already taken in the first of four Dash 8-300s ordered

scheduled/charter flights. Syktyvkar, based in the city of that name, has a vast fleet for regional and domestic passenger/cargo operations that includes over 40 Tu-134s and 25 An-2 biplanes; Tyumen Airlines of Siberia undertakes regional and domestic services with mostly Tu-154s among over 40 varied aircraft; Tyumenaviatrans Airline (and its subsidiaries in western Siberia) has access to a huge number of airliners, freighters and helicopters (including over 70 An-2 biplanes and 150 Mi-8 and Mi-17 helicopters) for domestic, regional and international services; the Ural Airline fleet at Ekaterinburg in the Urals includes four Il-86s and 20 Tu-154B/Ms; and Yakutaviatrans based at Yakutsk, Siberia, has over 50 airliners and freighters headed by 22 An-24s and ten or eleven Tu-154B/Ms.

Rwanda
This small African republic has three airports for scheduled flights. Operating out of the capital Kigali is the national airline, Rwandair, with a Twin Otter and 707-320C for passenger and cargo flights to two domestic destinations and Burundi, plus regional/international charters to Belgium, Tanzania, Uganda and Zaire.

São Tomé and Príncipe
These tiny islands off the west coast of Africa have a population of a little over 130,000. Two airports handle scheduled flights, with Air São Tomé e Príncipe as the flag carrier airline flying a single Twin Otter from its main base on São Tomé to Príncipe and Gabon, plus charter services. A much larger airline on São Tomé is Transafrik International, undertaking charter cargo flights in Africa using three L-100 Commercial Hercules and two 727 freighters.

Saudi Arabia
Saudi Arabian Airlines, known simply as Saudia, is the largest airline in the Middle East. It was founded in late 1946 by the Saudi Arabian Government, with technical assistance from TWA and the USAAF. Flights began on 14 March 1947.

Based at Jeddah, but with important hubs in Dhahran and the capital city of Riyadh (ar Riyād), it employs over 24,000 people and serves 25 domestic and over 50 international destinations. Its airliners and freighters total over 90 aircraft, when including 17 business jets of Cessna Citation, Dassault Falcon 900 and Gulfstream types, though in addition it has 16 lightplanes for other purposes. The main fleet is headed by 11 A300-600s, to which are added 23 747s, 19 TriStars, 20 737-200s and several lesser types. A modernization programme is currently introducing over 60 new aircraft into service, mainly in the form of large numbers of 777-200s and MD-90s, though also including five 747-400s and four MD-11s.

Saudi Arabian Airlines
Address: PO Box 620, CC 181,
21231 Jeddah, Saudi Arabia.
Telephone: +966 2 686 0000, 2349
Fax: +966 2 686 2006

Senegal
This republic on the west coast of Africa has two airports for scheduled flights. Air Senegal, owned mainly by the Government and Air Afrique, was founded in 1971 and currently flies two BAe 748s, a Dash 8 and a Twin Otter from the capital Dakar to five other domestic points and regional destinations in Cape Verde, Gambia and Guinea-Bissau. Other operations include charter and taxi work.

Seychelles
This island group in the Indian Ocean has a population of only about 75,000 and is served by two airports handling scheduled flights. The Government-owned national airline is Air Seychelles, an IATA member, which was founded in 1976. Based on the largest island of Mahé, which supports the capital city Victoria, it undertakes domestic flights and operates over important international routes to Dubai, France, Germany, India, Israel, Italy, Kenya, Singapore, South Africa, Spain, Switzerland and the UK. The fleet comprises two 767-200ER/-300ERs, one 757-200ER, four Twin Otters and an Islander.

Sierra Leone
Sierra National Airlines (IATA member) has a single 727-200 for flights out of the country's only airport for scheduled operations at Freetown, linking the capital cities of nearby Guinea, Ivory Coast, Ghana and Nigeria.

BELOW
An artist's impression of a Saudia 777-200

OPPOSITE,
ABOVE
Air Seychelles operates three modern extended-range Boeing 757/767s

OPPOSITE, BELOW
Singapore Airlines is the world's largest operator of Boeing 747-400 Megatops

Singapore

Two regional charter airlines are Air Mandalay, with three ATR 72s, and Region Air which has operated A310/A320s and two Dash 8s on an *ad hoc* basis although it was not listed as an Airbus user in August 1996, according to Airbus Industrie statistics.

Singapore Airlines (SIA), as the nation's flag carrier, was so named on 30 June 1972 following a decision by the governments of Malaysia and Singapore of January 1971 to set up separate airlines from Malaysia-Singapore Airlines Limited that ceased operations in October 1972. One of many highlights of SIA's past came in October 1977, when an agreement was signed with British Airways to operate joint regular Concorde services, starting that December.

With the age of its passenger aircraft averaging only five years and eight months in June 1996, the airline's total fleet then comprised 32 747-400 Megatops (plus one leased out; 14 more on firm order), five 747-300 Big Tops (plus three leased out), three 747-300 Combis, two 747-200s (plus two leased out), four 747-400 Mega Arks (two more on firm order), one 747-200 Freighter (plus one leased out), 17 A310-300s, six A310-200s, four A340-300E Celestars (two delivered in June 1996; 13 more on first order) and one DC-8-73 Freighter. Thirty-four 777s were then on firm order (six for Singapore Aircraft Leasing Enterprise – SALE) and 43 on option (including ten for SALE).

The SIA route network covers 73 cities in 41 countries, with four destinations in North America, 13 in Europe, ten in the South-West Pacific, 15 in North Asia, 13 in South-East Asia, and 18 in West Asia and Africa. SIA also operates freighter-only services to Chicago, Bangalore, Basel and Moscow. In addition, SIA's subsidiary SilkAir serves 20 destinations in eight Asian countries using five 737-300s and two Fokker 70s. During the latest full year, SIA carried 11,057,000 passengers, an increase of 9.7 per cent over the previous year, achieving 50,045.4 million RPK from 68,529.4 million ASK, a passenger seat factor of 73 per cent. Cargo load tonne-kilometre was then 3,820.1 million. The average number of employees for the year was 26,326.

Singapore Airlines Limited
Address: Airline House,
25 Airline Road, Singapore 819829.
Telephone: +65 542 3333
Fax: +65 545 6083

Slovakia

With four airports handling scheduled flights, the republic has Tatra Air as its flag airline, operating out of the capital Bratislava. Domestic services reach Kosice and international flights include the destinations of Prague and Zurich using Saab 340s.

Slovenia

This republic on the Adriatic has one airport for scheduled flights at the capital Ljubljana. Adria Airways was established in 1961 as a charter company, introducing scheduled flights and becoming an IATA member in the 1980s. Today, its scheduled and charter flights link the capital with 40 destinations in 17 countries, mostly in Europe. Since the independence of Slovenia on 25 June 1991, Adria has been the national airline. As a consequence, it was grounded shortly after by the Civil Aviation Authority of Yugoslavia for three months due to political reasons, but resumed operations at the end of January 1992 on the reduced market.

The Adria fleet comprises three A320s (two more ordered), two DC-9-30s and two Dash 7s, though it plans to phase out the two DC-9s in 1998 and replace them with modern Stage 3 aircraft. It has 697 employees, of whom 180 are flight crew. In the latest full year it carried 547,511 passengers, recording an accumulated distance of 5,631,485 miles (9,063,000 km).

Adria Airways
Address: Kuzmiceva 7, 1000 Ljubljana, Slovenia.
Telephone: +386 61 13 34 336
Fax: +386 61 323 356

Solomon Islands

The Government-owned national carrier is Solomon Airlines (IATA member), founded in 1962. Based at the capital Honiara, it currently links domestic points plus destinations in Australia, Efate, New Zealand and Papua New Guinea. In addition to a 737, it flies two Islanders and two Twin Otters.

Somalia

Somalia has a single airport for scheduled flights. Somali Airlines has not operated its two Dornier 228s since 1991 but is expected to begin again at a future date.

South Africa

Of the twenty or so noteworthy South African airlines, Commercial Airways (Comair), Safair, South African Airways, Sun Air and TREK Airways are all IATA members.

Commercial Airways, better known simply as Comair, is South Africa's longest established and largest private airline, starting operations on 14 July 1946. It provides over 270 flights each week from Johannesburg International Airport to destinations in southern Africa, using a fleet of six 737-200s, four Fokker F27s and two ATR 42s. Apart from domestic destinations, the route network extends to Swaziland, Botswana, Zimbabwe and Namibia.

In the latest full year, Comair carried more than 700,000 passengers. This is expected to rise to over one million by the end of 1996. In addition to scheduled flights, it offers inclusive Fly-in Safari packages to the Kruger National Park and adjoining game reserves.

In June 1996 Comair announced that it had signed a franchise agreement with British Airways, allowing it (from September) to provide a high-quality business class service at competitive fares. While remaining independent under existing local management, it uses the British Airways name and livery and its aircraft are being converted and upgraded to meet BA standards, while other operating benefits are being gained.

Commercial Airways (Comair)
Address: 1 Marignane Drive (PO Box 7015),
Cnr Atlas Road, Bonaero Park 1622,
South Africa.
Telephone: +27 11 921 0111
Fax: +27 11 973 3913, 1659

Safair is a worldwide charter airline headquartered at

Johannesburg International Airport also handling aircraft leasing. It is a wholly-owned subsidiary of Safmarine, a shipping line of the Safren Group, and has operated since 1969. It currently flies nine L-100-30 Commercial Hercules freighters, six 727-200Advs in passenger configuration and a Partenavia P68. Unusual assignments have included shipment of an oil rig in the Arctic, search and rescue operations, United Nations logistical support, aerial delivery, outsized cargoes, and oil spill spraying.

Safair
Address: PO Box 938, Kempton Park 1620,
South Africa.
Telephone: +27 11 395 0000
Fax: +27 11 395 1314

South African Airways is the Government-owned national airline, founded in February 1934 and absorbing Union Airways of 1929 establishment. Currently serving the domestic cities of Johannesburg, Bloemfontein, Durban, Cape Town, Port Elizabeth, East London and George (about 575 flights weekly), it also has an international network (85 flights each week) to seven European cities, five in the Far East, New York and Miami in North America, Rio de Janeiro and São Paulo in South America, two in Australia, and Israel and Dubai in the Middle East, plus a regional network to 12 African and Indian Ocean island destinations (72 flights each week).

The present SAA fleet comprises 48 aircraft, although this includes a Junkers Ju 52 for promotions and charters, a DC-3 and a DC-4 for charters, and a Harvard for air shows as the airline's Historic Flight Section. The main fleet for airline operations encompasses four 747-400s, two 747-300s, five 747-200s, one 747-200 freighter, four 747SPs, one 767, eight A300s, seven A320s, and 13 737-200s. Four 777-200s were ordered in November 1995 for delivery from 1997 (with options for three more) and SAA later announced its intention to purchase two more 747-400s. Among its other interests can be counted SA Express, a domestic commuter airline with 12 Dash 8s, in which SAA has a 20 per cent shareholding.

South African Airways
Address: SAA Towers, Wolmarans Street, Braamfontein,
Johannesburg 2001, South Africa.
Telephone: +27 11 773 9003
Fax: +27 11 773 9858

Sun Air was previously known as Bop Air, taking its

new identity from the reincorporation of Bophuthatswana into South Africa in April 1994. It operates as a domestic carrier on the 'Golden Triangle', linking the key business and tourist destinations of Cape Town, Durban and Johannesburg and carrying about 500,000 passengers each year. The fleet comprises five DC-9-32s, two 727-200s and a Citation 550.

Sun Air
Address: Private Bag 145,
Johannesburg International Airport,
1627, South Africa.
Telephone: +27 11 397 2233
Fax: +27 11 397 2234

Spain

Of eighteen or more noteworthy airlines in Spain, six are IATA members. Air España SA (IATA member) was founded in February 1984 and carried its first passengers on charter flights in November 1986 under the commercial operating name Air Europa. Initially part of a tourism and air transport group based in the UK, a group of Spanish investors purchased most of the capital stock in 1991 and it is today one of the most important private airlines in Europe.

Charter flights continue in central and northern Europe and further afield to destinations which include Thailand, Brazil, Cuba and the Dominican Republic, but in November 1993 it began scheduled services from Madrid and Barcelona to the Canary and Balearic Islands, adding a Madrid-Barcelona service in January 1994, and London and New York in November 1995. The national scheduled network now takes in 18 destinations (including Gran Canaria, Tenerife and other island destinations). The total number of passengers carried in the latest full year was 4,323,926.

Air Europa has ten 737-300s, five 737-400s and seven 757-200s, all leased, plus a 767-200 that joined the fleet in April 1996. Between November 1998 and the year 2000 the airline plans to take in ten 737-800s. The current employment level is 1,601, when including 619 in the self-handling division and the airline's 748 direct and 234 indirect personnel, of which 217 are pilots.

Air Europa
Address: Gran Via Asima, 23,
Polígono Son Castelló,
07009 – Palma de Mallorca, Spain.
Telephone: +34 71 178 100
Fax: +34 71 431 500

Aviaco (Aviación y Comercio S.A.), headquartered in Madrid and an IATA member, is principally concerned with domestic scheduled and charter flights, although foreign destinations take in Stansted (UK) and Paris (France). It has a large fleet of 33 MD-88s and DC-9s.

Aviaco is partly owned by Iberia (32.93 per cent), which is the national airline of Spain and an IATA member (shareholders are Teneo 99.83 per cent and others 0.17 per cent). The Iberia fleet comprises four DC-9s, five A300s, 22 A320-200s, two A340s, 24 MD-87s, seven DC-10s, 28 727s, eight 757s, seven 747s and three DC-8s for passenger and cargo operations, while six more A340s and eight A321s are on order.

With its main bases in Barcelona and Madrid and a hub in Miami, it operates to 24 European,

LEFT
One of five Sun Air McDonnell Douglas DC-9-32s

BOTTOM
Iberia McDonnell Douglas MD-87

OPPOSITE
One of three Adria Airways Airbus A320s

BELOW
SA Express Dash 8 Series 300 B

Viva's fleet of nine 737-300s (majority leased) carried 962,001 passengers in the latest full year. The airline employs 458 persons, including 71 pilots and co-pilots.

Viva air
Address: Calle Zurbano, 41 – 28010 Madrid, Spain.
Telephone: +34 1 349 06 00
Fax: +34 1 349 06 13

Air Nostrum is another IATA airline, operating Fokker 50s on scheduled domestic and regional services. The sixth IATA airline is Spanair, founded in 1986 and owned by the Spanish Travel Agency Viajes Marsans (51 per cent) and SAS (49 per cent). It began flying as a charter airline in March 1988, adding scheduled domestic services from March 1994. Today it connects the Spanish mainland and the Canary and Baleares Islands to more than 100 airports in Europe, the USA and Central America, carrying 3,304,052 passengers in the latest full year and recording an accumulated RPK of nearly 1,750.5 million. Employees then totalled 1,283.

Spanair
Address: Aeropuerto de Palma, Apdo 50086, 07000 Palma de Mallorca, Spain.
Telephone: +34 (9) 71 49 20 12
Fax: +34 (9) 71 49 25 53

27 intercontinental and seven other foreign destinations plus ten domestic cities (when including its bases), with an average of 413 flights each day. A total of 13,665,000 passengers was carried in the latest full year, split as 6,627,000 within Spain, 5,644,000 throughout the rest of Europe and 1,754,000 over intercontinental routes. Employees then stood at 23,245, including 1,165 pilots.

Iberia was founded on 14 December 1927 with three Rohrbach Roland aircraft flying between Madrid and Barcelona. It was granted the monopoly for domestic air travel in 1943 and on 22 September 1946 opened transatlantic flights from Madrid to Buenos Aires with a DC-4, the first of several transatlantic routes to be established over the next few years. Today, it also has substantial interests in other airlines including Aviaco, Aérolineas Argentinas (83.35 per cent, though likely to change), Ladeco (37.35 per cent), Viasa (45 per cent), Viva air, Binter Canarias (99.99 per cent) to exploit regional services in the Canary Islands, and Cargosur (100 per cent) for air mail and cargo work, the final three newly-founded Spanish airlines being incorporated into the Iberia Group in 1988, joined in 1989 by Binter Mediterráneo (99.99 per cent).

Iberia
Address: Velazquez, 130 – 28006 Madrid, Spain.
Telephone: +34 1 587 87 87
Fax: +34 1 587 73 29

Viva air (IATA member) was itself originally launched as a joint venture between Iberia and Lufthansa, on 4 February 1988, inaugurating services with a flight between Palma de Mallorca and Nuremburg on 15 April 1988. Until 1990 it was fundamentally a charter airline operating some additional scheduled flights on behalf of Iberia, but then the decision was taken to transform it into a scheduled operator, with a minimum of charter work, using Iberia's designator code until 1991. Iberia also took over the majority of shares (96 per cent).

Some scheduled flights for Iberia continued until 1994, though most work was by then its own. Then, on 1 February 1995, it relinquished its profitable Middle East and African network to Iberia, followed soon after by all its scheduled routes, returning to charter status for Spanish and European operators.

Sri Lanka

Airlanka began scheduled operations on 1 September 1979 using two leased 707s, with the Sri Lanka Government Treasury, Bank of Ceylon and People's Bank providing initial funding and Singapore Airlines offering management assistance until 1981. It is the national airline, also handling all air cargo movements in and out of the country using its cargo complex and warehouse area.

The airline flies to 31 destinations in 22 countries from its base at Bandaranaike International Airport in Katunayake, including Europe, South Africa, the Middle East, the Indian sub-continent, South-East Asia, the Far East and the Maldives. It uses three A340-300s, two A320-200s, two L-1011-500 TriStars, one L-1011-100 TriStar and one L-1011-50 TriStar. A total of 1,198,248 passengers was carried in the latest full year.

Airlanka
Address: 37 York Street, Colombo 01, Sri Lanka.
Telephone: +94 1 73 5555
Fax: +94 1 73 5122

A small domestic airline is Lionair, which began operating in 1994 and has four An-24s.

Sudan

Of five principal airlines, only the Government-owned Sudan Airways, headquartered at Khartoum, is an IATA member. Founded in 1946, it initially received technical and flying assistance from the British company, Airwork, expanding services over its borders to take in Cairo by late 1954 and joining the jet age in 1959 with the introduction of a Viscount service to London.

Today it has a fleet of one owned A320, a leased A310 and a leased A300, two Fokker 50s, two 737-200Cs, a small number of 707-300Cs and three Twin Otters. In addition to its domestic network, it flies to

19 regional and international destinations and employs over 2,300 persons. The yearly passenger-mile total is over 382 million (615 million passenger-km).

Sudan Airways Company
Address: SDC Building, ST-15 New Extension, PO Box 253, Khartoum, Sudan.
Telephone: +249 11 47 953
Fax: +249 11 47 978

Suriname

With two airports handling scheduled flights, this small South American republic has Suriname Airways as its national airline (IATA member). It undertakes domestic and regional flights with a Dash 8, two Twin Otters and a Cessna 206 lightplane.

Swaziland

The single airport for scheduled flights at Manzini is the base for Royal Swazi National Airways (IATA member), a partly Government-owned airline with a Fokker 100 and an F28 for regional services to eight African destinations.

An international charter cargo airline headquartered at the administrative capital of Mbabane is Air Swazi Cargo, with a 707-320C.

Sweden

Of fifteen or thereabouts main airlines, only four are IATA members. Those that are not members include Transwede Airways, a scheduled and charter carrier with ten 757s, Fokker 100s and MD-87s for domestic and international services, though some aircraft are on lease to other operators.

Falcon Aviation undertakes both scheduled and charter flights, using three 737-300 quick-change airliners that can be converted between passenger and cargo configurations. Also headquartered at Malmö-

Sturup is Malmö Aviation Schedule, which has a fleet of some 15 BAe 146s and similar Avro International RJ85s for its European passenger and cargo services, including a few QT Quiet Traders.

The national airline of Sweden, Norway and Denmark is Scandinavian Airlines System (SAS), a consortium in which DDL (*see* Denmark) has a two-sevenths stake. DNL (*see* Norway) has a similar stake, and SILA and ABA (Swedish Intercontinental Airlines and Swedish Airlines) of Sweden jointly have a three-sevenths stake. In each case, the constituent companies are equally owned by their respective States and private shareholders. The SAS consortium itself has shareholdings in various affiliated companies, including British Midland (40 per cent), Spanair (49 per cent), Grønlandsfly (37.5 per cent) and airBaltic (28.51 per cent).

DDL had been founded in 1918, ABA in 1924, DNL in 1927 and SILA in 1943, and it was SILA which undertook the first post-Second World War civil flight between Europe and the USA (on 27 June 1945) using a commercialized Flying Fortress that had been modified by Saab. However, on 1 August 1946 DDL, DNL and SILA established SAS to operate intercontinental services, with the inaugural flight by a DC-4 to New York on 17 September and to South America on 30 November. On 18 April 1948 DDL, DNL and ABA founded European SAS (ESAS) to co-ordinate European services using DC-6s, and on 1 July ABA and SILA merged. In 1954 SAS became the first airline to fly a scheduled Polar route, between Copenhagen and Los Angeles. On 10 April 1996 SAS and United Airlines began code-share operations on a total of 66 combined European, transatlantic and US domestic routes.

In the latest full operating year, SAS carried 18.9 million passengers to 105 destinations in 34 countries, a destinations total that has since increased to include Bologna (Italy), Newcastle (UK), further US cities and others. It employs some 21,000 persons and has approximately 154 aircraft in its fleet, namely 13 767s, one 747-200SF cargo, 31 MD-81s, 12 MD-82s, two MD-83s, 18 MD-87s, 34 DC-9s, 22 Fokker 50s, 19 F28s and two 737-300QCs. In addition, the first of eight MD-90s were to join the airline in late 1996. It has also ordered 41 737-600s, with an option for 35 more, for delivery from 1998 to gradually replace DC-9s and F28s. The F28s and Fokker 50s are operated by SAS Commuter (*see* Denmark).

Scandinavian Airlines System (SAS)
Address: S-195 87 Stockholm, Sweden.
Telephone: +46 8 797 0000
Fax: +46 8 797 1515

Skyways, based at Linköpings Airport and owned by Salénia AB, is Sweden's leading domestic airline in terms of destinations, carrying nearly 600,000 passengers a year. It operates 12 Saab 340s and five Fokker 50s to 20 domestic and international points and employs some 224 persons.

Although it took its present name in 1993, the company has its origins in the Avia airline that was formed in 1940 and performed target towing flights during the Second World War, adding cropspraying, taxi flights and crew training in 1945. In December 1986 it began scheduled airline services under the ownership of the Gotlandsbolaget shipping company. That same year Salénia took over the bankrupt airline AMA Flyg, which in January 1987 was launched as Salair. One year later, Avia purchased Golden Air and Salair bought Skyways of Scandinavia, and in 1992 the two airlines merged under the name Avia. However, Salénia bought out its co-owner in 1993, changing the airline's name to Skyways and focusing operations at Stockholm's Arlanda Airport.

Skyways
Address: Box 1537, 581 15 Linköping, Sweden.
Telephone: +46 13 37 55 00
Fax: +46 13 37 55 01

Switzerland

Swiss Air Transport, better known as Swissair, is the national carrier, voted 'Airline of the Year' in 1996. It was founded on 26 March 1931, following the merger of Balair and Ad Astra, and, interestingly, it employed the first air hostesses in Europe in 1934. In 1935 it took in the famed Douglas DC-2, with DC-3s being acquired from 1936 (the last DC-3 was not withdrawn from revenue service until 1964).

Having suspended scheduled operations during the Second World War, Swissair became the designated national airline of Switzerland in 1947, with 30 per cent of shares held by Swiss public institutions. It entered the jet age in 1960 with receipt of DC-8s and Caravelles, becoming an all-jet fleet by 1968. The airline's 100 millionth passenger was carried in 1982.

In 1991 Swissair acquired majority voting rights in the regional carrier, Crossair (*see later*), while on 7 April 1995 the subsidiary, Swissair Asia, began services to T'aipei using a single MD-11. In the same year the Swissair Board resolved to incorporate the charter operations of Balair/CTA into Swissair (long haul) and Crossair (short haul), transferring its remaining scheduled services with aircraft of up to 100 seats to Crossair's operation. Swissair also signed an agreement with Sabena and the Belgium Government, laying the foundations for closer collaboration between the two airlines, with Swissair

acquiring a 49.5 per cent holding in Sabena. Swissair also concluded a co-operation accord with Transwede.

The Swissair route network takes in 127 cities in 71 countries when including joint-venture services performed by partner airlines (which include Austrian Airlines and Delta Air Lines), one of the latest being Vancouver from 15 June 1996. Its fleet comprised in the summer of 1996 six Fokker 100s, 13 MD-81s, 12 A320s, three A319s (latest delivered in August 1996; others on order), six A321s, eight A310-300s, 13 MD-11s and five 747-357s (three Combis), with four A319s, six A320s, and three MD-11s on order. In the latest full year it carried 8,406,977 passengers and 301,774 tons (306,617 tonnes) of cargo and mail. The average number of employees for the period was 16,117.

Swiss Air Transport (Swissair)
Address: Hirschengarben 84,
CH-8001 Zürich, Sweden.
Telephone: +41 1 812 12 12
Fax: +41 1 810 80 46

Crossair was founded in 1975 as a private airline but is now the regional carrier of the Swissair Group, with Swissair having acquired a 38 per cent holding in 1988 and majority voting rights in 1991. Its route network has been expanding rapidly and its aircraft perform services for the company itself and for its parent airline, the fleet increasing from 36 to 49 aircraft during 1995 alone, while in 1996 16 new Saab 2000s, Avro RJ100s and MD-82s were joining the fleet. In July 1996, eight MD-82/83s, four RJ85s, 11 RJ100s, 16 Saab 340s and 20 Saab 2000s were in operation.

OPPOSITE
Airlanka Airbus A340-300

ABOVE
Scandinavian Airlines System (SAS) Boeing 767-300 (Ted Fahn)

INSET
One of Air Tahiti's three ATR 42s

Crossair has recently assumed responsibility for
all scheduled services involving aircraft of up to 100
seats within the Swissair Group and the assimilation
of the short-haul charter flights of the former
Balair/CTA. It flies to over 77 destinations (not
including charter) in 26 European countries, carrying
3 million scheduled passengers a year. Over 2,000
persons are employed.

Crossair
Address: Postfach, CH-4002 Basel, Sweden.
Telephone: +41 61 325 25 25
Fax: +41 61 325 32 68

Syria

Syria has five airports for scheduled flights. The
Government-owned IATA national carrier is Syrian
Arab Airlines (Syrianair), founded in 1961 and
operating scheduled services to three domestic cities
plus destinations in the Middle East, the Far East,
North Africa and Europe. Its 17 aircraft include three
Tu-154Ms, six 727-200s and two 747SPs.

Syrian Arab Airlines
Address: Youssef Al Azmen Square,
PO Box 417, Damascus, Syrian Arab Republic.
Telephone: +963 11 23 1838
Fax: +963 11 23 2154

Tahiti

Tahiti has three domestic airlines, including Tahiti
Conquest Airlines and Air Tahiti, of which the latter
is the largest and an IATA member. Air Tahiti has its
origins in Régie Aérienne Interinsulaire (RAI), which
had taken over the semi-charter services of the
original Air Tahiti and TRAPAS, and in 1953 had
begun scheduled flights between Tahiti and Bora-
Bora, followed by Raiatea. After a merger and a
name change, the Polynesian branch of the airline
became Air Polynésie, which in 1987 was again
renamed as Air Tahiti.

Air Tahiti's route network takes in the
Windward and Leeward Islands, North Tuamotu
islands, the Marquesas, East Tuamotu (Gambier) and
the Australes Islands. It operates three ATR 72-200s,
three ATR 42-300s, a Dornier 228-212 and a TO 300,

although three ATR 42-500s (for November 1996 to
December 1997 delivery) are replacing the ATR 42-
300s. In the latest full year the airline carried 418,819
passengers on regular flights, accumulating 132.529
million RPK.

Air Tahiti
Address: Airport of Tahiti Faaa,
BP 314 Papeete, Tahiti, French Polynesia.
Telephone: +689 86 40 00
Fax: +689 86 40 69

The third airline is Air Moorea, a branch of Air
Tahiti (55 per cent shareholding) created to serve the
island of Moorea, offering large numbers of daily
round trips by small capacity aircraft (plus charters).
Employing 70 staff, it carries 160,000 passengers
yearly using six Islanders, two Twin Otters, two Piper
Aztecs and a Chieftain.

Taiwan

Taiwan has a number of substantial airlines,
including EVA Airways with nine 767s, ten 747-400s

and six MD-11s (plus 747-400s on order), and its
subsidiary, Makung International Airlines, with
MD-90s, five BAe 146s and a 757 in its fleet; Far
Eastern Air Transport (FAT) with 16 aircraft
including MD-82/83s, 757s and 737s; Formosa
Airlines with mostly turboprop types, though
including two new Fokker 100s; Great China Airlines
operating Dash 8s but with three MD-90s ordered;
Taiwan Airlines with Islanders and Trislanders;
TransAsia Airways with six A320s, four A321s
(latest delivered on 15 July 1996; two more ordered),
and 15 ATR 42/72s; and U-Land Airlines with a few
MD-82s.

The nation's flag carrier is China Airlines,
which has Mandarin Airlines as a wholly-owned
subsidiary operating a 747-400 to Australia, New
Zealand and Canada. China Airlines was founded on
16 December 1959 by a group of retired air force
specialists becoming the country's first air carrier
fully owned by Chinese. In 1961 it was asked to
parachute supplies into Laos and in 1962 was
contracted to fly for the Vietnamese Government and
the US military, providing the finance to open its first

domestic scheduled services and, in 1966, its first
international route (to Saigon).

Today, China Airlines flies passengers and cargo
to more than 30 destinations in 17 countries of Asia,
Europe, North America, Africa and the Oceania,
using 13 A300s, two A320s, four MD-11s, 20 747s
(four firm orders plus four options placed for more
747-400s in May 1996, for delivery from May 1997
to 2002) and three 737s (six 737-800s ordered, with
nine options, for delivery from 1998). In the latest
full year, it transported 6,472,000 passengers,
accumulating an RPK of 17,083 million, plus over
656 million pounds (nearly 298 million kg) of cargo.
It also has a 10 per cent shareholding in FAT. It
adopted a new livery in October 1995.

China Airlines
Address: 131, Nanking E. Road,
Sec. 3, T'aipei, Taiwan, R.O.C.
Telephone: +886 2 7152233
Fax: +886 2 5145419

Tajikistan
This republic, formerly part of the USSR, has a
single airport for scheduled flights. Tajikistan
International Airlines began flying in 1995 between
the capital of Dushanbe and London using a fleet of
bought and leased TriStars (a 767-200 is on order).

Tanzania
With eleven airports for scheduled flights, this East
African country has Air Tanzania Corporation (IATA
member) as its flag airline (mainly Government
owned), founded in 1977 to take over routes from the
former East African Airways (founded 1946). Both
scheduled and charter flights are operated on a
domestic and regional basis, using two 737-200Cs
and two F27s.

Thailand
Founded for air-taxi operations in 1968, Sahakol
Air expanded into scheduled services in 1986 and
three years later took its present name, Bangkok
Airways. Today, still as a private concern, it has a
fleet of about nine turboprop airlines (including two
ATR 72s and three Dash 8s) for its domestic and
regional scheduled services, plus flights to holiday

destinations.

The national airline is Thai Airways
International, which can trace its lineage to the
former regional/domestic airline, Thai Airways
Company. TAC had been founded in 1951 by the
merger of two earlier regional carriers in an attempt
to end route duplication. On 14 December 1958
Scandinavian Airlines System took a 30 per cent
holding in TAC, supplying its unwanted but still
modern piston airliners to help establish Thai
International in 1959. This also had the effect of
opening up the Far East to the European partner.
Services began on 1 May 1960. The association
lasted until 1977. Thai International and TAC finally
joined forces in 1988.

Today Thai Airways International is mostly
owned by the Thai Government. It operates an
extensive international/regional network to 36
countries in Asia, the Middle/Far East, Australia,
North America and Europe, while maintaining full
domestic services. Its large fleet incorporates four
turboprop ATR 42/72s but is otherwise pure-jet,

headed by two A310s, 19 A300s and eight A330s.
The remainder of the fleet comprises the first few of
14 777-200/-300s ordered (the first 777s with Rolls-
Royce engines; first entering commercial service in
June 1996) and some 17 747-200/-300/-400s (three
747-400s ordered), seven 737-400s, five BAe 146s,
four MD-11s and any DC-10s.

Thai Airways International
Address: 89 Vibhavadi Rangsit Road,
10900 Bangkok, Thailand.
Telephone: +66 2 5130121
Fax: +66 2 5122135

Tonga
An IATA member, Royal Tongan Airlines was
established in November 1985, originally as Friendly
Islands Airways and flying a C-212 and Islander. The
airline began to improve the Ha'apai and Vava'u
airfields for better domestic services (there are now
six domestic airports) and in 1986 used its C-212 to

inaugurate its first international route, to Pago Pago.

In July 1991 the airline adopted its present name, while also commencing a seat-sharing arrangement to Auckland using a Solomon Airlines 737. By then the C-212 had been deleted from the fleet and two Twin Otters added (1987), allowing the airline to concentrate on better outer island services.

Today, the airline flies to Auckland (New Zealand), Sydney (Australia), Nadi and Suva (Fiji), Honolulu (Hawaii – code-share with Air New Zealand), Los Angeles/San Francisco (USA – code-share with Air New Zealand), Alofi (Niue) and Apia (Western Samoa), using a 737 and BAe 748. Another international station is in the UK. The same BAe 748 plus the Twin Otters are used for its domestic schedules.

Royal Tongan Airlines
Address: Royco Building, Fatafehi Road,
Private Bag 9, Nuku'alofa, Tonga.
Telephone: +676 23 004
Fax: +676 24 056

Trinidad and Tobago

The new BWIA International Airways Limited was incorporated on 15 February 1995, with privatization completed on the 22nd of that month when the Government turned over majority control of the common stock and management to private US and Caribbean investors, though retaining a 33.5 per cent interest. However, BWIA actually has a history that goes back to 1940.

BWIA (British West Indian Airways) was founded on 27 November 1940, when Captain Lowell Yerex began a daily service between Trinidad and Barbados and Tobago using a Lockheed Lodestar. In 1947 the airline was bought by British South American Airways and was temporarily renamed British International Airways, but in 1949 BSAA itself amalgamated with BOAC, the British national airline, making BWIA a BOAC subsidiary. Further change came on 1 November 1961 when the Government of Trinidad and Tobago purchased BWIA from BOAC, allowing the latter to re-purchase a 10 per cent holding, though even this was re-acquired in 1968.

In January 1980, BWIA merged with Trinidad & Tobago Air Services to form Trinidad and

Tobago (BWIA International) Airways Corporation, while restructuring commenced in 1991 to facilitate the changeover from a state-owned corporation to a public company. A BWIA Express operation was announced in May 1995 for turboprop feeder flights, combining the services of three regional airlines, namely Cardinal Airlines of Dominica, Carib Aviation of Antigua and Trans Island Air of Barbados, to connect 19 other island destinations via the BWIA gateways of Antigua and Barbados.

The current BWIA fleet comprises one A321 (two A340s ordered), six L-1011-500 TriStars and four MD-83s. In the latest full year, 951,244 passengers were carried, while 2,376 staff were employed. The route network encompasses Antigua, Barbados, Grenada, Jamaica, St Lucia, St Maarten, and Trinidad and Tobago in the Caribbean; London, Frankfurt and Zurich in Europe; Georgetown and Caracas in South America; and Miami, New York and Toronto in North America.

BWIA International Airways Limited
Address: Golden Grove Road, Piarco,
Port of Spain, Trinidad and Tobago.
Telephone: +809 669 3000
Fax: +809 669 1865

Tunisia

Of several airlines operating in Tunisia, only Tunisair (Société Tunisienne de l'Air) is an IATA member, founded by the Government and Air France in 1948. Employing over 7,000 staff, the airline has a current fleet of eight A320s, one A300, eight 737-200/-500s and up to eight 727-200s, offering flights from Tunis to some 13 countries in the Middle East, Africa and Europe.

Turkey

Turkey has about a dozen airlines operating large aircraft, including the charter carriers Air Alfa with five A300s within its fleet; Birgenair with a 767 and 737; Istanbul Airlines with two 757s, six 737s and eight 727s; Onur Air Tasimacilik with five A320s, three A321s and two A300s (MD-88s ordered); and Sunways Intersun Havacilik with three MD-83s.

The national airline is Turkish Airlines (Turk Hava Yollari – THY), which counts the tourist charter airline SunExpress Air as a subsidiary (five 737s). Turkish Airlines itself was founded in Ankara on 30 May 1933 as part of the Ministry of Defence, under the name 'State Airlines Administration'. It was renamed Turkish Airlines Co. Inc. in 1955, after gaining a new organizational status. A service to Singapore in 1986 inaugurated its Far East routes and

a New York service from 1988 opened up North America.

A limited privatization took place from 22 August 1990, when some shares were offered to the public, and the airline continues with the Government holding 98.2 per cent of shares. Promulgation of the law on 27 November 1994 concerning changes in privatization procedures redefined Turkish Airlines as a State Enterprise under the jurisdiction of the Privatization Administration.

Currently, THY uses seven A310-203s, seven A310-304s, three leased A320-200s, four A340-300s, 28 737-400s, two 737-500s, ten RJ100s, four RJ70s, and three 727-200F freighters. A new A340-311 will be delivered in 1997. In the latest full year 8,599,250 passengers were carried, with an accumulated distance flown of 64,012,337 miles (103,017,903 km). Its route network covers 26 domestic and 56 international destinations, with 33 in Europe, 11 in the Middle East, nine in the Far East, two in Africa and one in the USA.

Turkish Airlines
Address: Genel Yönetim Binasi,
Atatürk Havalimani, Yesilköy,
34830 Istanbul, Turkey.
Telephone: +90 212 663 63 00
Fax: +90 212 663 47 44

Turkmenistan

This republic, formerly part of the USSR, has one airport at Ashkhabad handling scheduled flights. The national airline is Turkmenistan Airlines, offering domestic and regional scheduled/charter services with a mixed Russian, Ukrainian and Western fleet of aircraft comprising some 30 An-24s, Tu-154Bs and Yak-42s, plus two Il-76TD freighters, three 757s, three 737s, a business jet and various Mil helicopters.

Krasnovodsk Airline at Krasnovodsk Airport operates about 13 An-24s and An-26s.

Turks and Caicos Islands

These island groups in the British West Indies, situated between the Bahamas and Dominican Republic, east of Cuba, have Turks and Caicos Airways as the flag airline, headquartered at Providenciales in Caicos. It operates a small number of turboprop aircraft for domestic and regional scheduled services, including EMB-120 Brasilias, Islanders, Piper Aztecs, a Twin Otter and a Beech 1900C.

Uganda

With a single airport situated at Entebbe near the capital Kampala, Uganda has few and limited indigenous air transport companies. Indeed, its largest airline, Das Air Cargo, has the UK's Gatwick Airport as the main hub for its cargo operations, flying to 19 cities in East and West Africa, while Entebbe, Accra and Nairobi are its primary bases for return flights to Europe. Its main cargoes are flowers and pineapples.

Das Air Cargo is the trading name for the airline activities of the Ugandan company Dairo Air Services. It has a fleet of four 707F freighters fitted with hushkits and a DC-10-30F (two more DC-10-30F freighters are to follow in 1997 and 1999), plus sub-leased aircraft to maintain regularity of services. Formed in 1983 and initially operating *ad hoc* charters between Africa and Europe using a 707 freighter, the scheduled part of Das Air Cargo's

charter services began in 1985. Today, 60 people are employed. Das Air Cargo USA is also part of the company operating from Orlando, from where traffic is fed on interline arrangements from the major American intercontinental gateways to connect with Das African services from London, though Das Air Cargo does hold the necessary FAA approvals to operate direct from the USA.

Das Air Cargo
Address: ANA House, Aviation Court,
Gatwick Road, Crawley, Sussex RH10 2RJ, UK.
Telephone: +44 1293 540303, 545945
Fax: +44 1293 514036, 551545

A scheduled passenger and cargo airline headquartered in Uganda is Alliance, founded in 1994 with assistance from South African Airways, which is a major shareholder and supplier of the single wet-leased 747SP. Bombay in India and Gatwick in the UK are major destinations. The Tanzanian and Ugandan governments and their respective national airlines also hold important interests.

Uganda Airlines is the wholly Government-owned national carrier, founded in 1976 and operating two 737s and an F27. Its regional services take in some nine African and Middle East points.

Ukraine

The vast republic of Ukraine has 20 airports handling scheduled flights and a developing air network. Home of the Antonov Design Bureau which produces a range of military and civil transports (most importantly freighters), it is hardly surprising that many Ukrainian airlines are charter cargo carriers, though Russian-built Il-76s can also be regularly found in the fleets. Indeed, Antonov itself has established its own niche in the worldwide cargo charter business, initially by working with Britain's Air Foyle as its worldwide general sales agent in the commercial exploitation of the giant An-124 freighter but more recently by marketing its own services and offering use of a range of its own aircraft from the elderly An-12 through to the world's largest aircraft, the six-jet An-225.

Other Ukrainian charter cargo airlines include Air Navigation Transport Agency, Air Service

Ukraine, Antonov Airtrak (also an An-124 operator), Khors Air, Lana Air and Vitair, while charter airlines offering passenger flights (often also cargo) include BSL Airlines, Odessa Airline and UNA. In addition, Atlant SV Airlines offers both scheduled passenger and charter cargo operations with a huge fleet.

Antonov transports also feature widely in the ranks of the other airlines offering scheduled flights, including Air Urga, Crimea Krymavia Airline and Dneproavia. Alternatively, Ukraine International Airlines (which is mainly Government owned) has three Boeing 737s for domestic services and flights throughout Europe.

The only IATA airline is Air Ukraine, the nation's flag carrier which includes Dneproavia and the domestic/regional Lvov among its subsidiaries. Indeed, it handles all of the Government's interests held in Ukrainian airlines and airports. Based at Kiev, its route network includes domestic points and international flights to the Czech Republic, Ireland, and four cities in North America.

The Air Ukraine fleet is truly astonishing, with some 200 aircraft which range from a couple of old remaining Il-18s to some 80 An-24/-26/-30/-32/-72s, more than 30 Tu-154B/Ms, well over 20 Tu-134s, plus Yak 40/-42s, Ilyushin Il-62Ms, a handful of Boeing 737s and Czech-built L-410s.

Air Ukraine
Address: 14 Avenue Peremogy,
252135 Kiev, Ukraine.
Telephone: +380 44 216 7109
Fax: +380 44 216 8235

BELOW
Das Air Cargo McDonnell Douglas DC-10-30F freighter for its African services

OPPOSITE,
ABOVE
The first of the newly acquired Boeing 777s for Thai Airways International

OPPOSITE,
BELOW
Airbus A310 belonging to Turkish Airlines

United Arab Emirates

Of the five or so noteworthy UAE airlines, only Emirates is an IATA member. Of the others, Daallo Airlines flies one Tu-154M plus eight turboprop aircraft and Oman Aviation Services has two A320s plus some six small jets and turboprop aircraft.

The flag airline of the UAE is Emirates Airlines, wholly owned by the Government of Dubai but representing the UAE nations. Founded in 1985, it offers scheduled domestic and international passenger services to nearly 40 destinations in Asia, Africa, Europe, the Middle and Far East, the Comoros, Indonesia and Australia, plus freight operations to Singapore. It has a fleet of ten A310-300s, six A300-600Rs and three 777s (four more ordered plus seven options), and accumulates in excess of 3,975 million passenger-miles (6,397 million passenger-km) yearly.

Emirates Airlines
Address: PO Box 686, Dubai, UAE.
Telephone: +971 4 283848
Fax: +971 4 227969

United Kingdom

Over 60 airlines operate from the UK, including 12 that are members of IATA. These are Air UK, British Airways, British Midland Airways, British Regional Airlines, Business Air at Dyce in Aberdeen (eight Saab 340s and a BAe 146-200) for scheduled and charter services in Britain and to Esbjerg (Denmark) and Frankfurt (Germany), GB Airways at Gatwick Airport for international scheduled passenger/cargo flights as a British Airways' franchise airline (737s – *see* British Airways), Gill Airways, Hunting Cargo Airlines, Jersey European Airways, Maersk Air (*see* Denmark), Manx Airlines and Virgin Atlantic Airways.

British Regional Airlines was formed on 27 October 1996 by the merger of Loganair at Glasgow Airport and Manx Airlines (Europe) on the Isle of Man, becoming one of Europe's largest commuter airlines and operating as another British Airways' franchise airline under the British Airways Express banner (*see* P. 69 Manx Airlines). Loganair brought a fleet of seven Shorts 360s, five Islanders and a Twin Otter (modified to Series 310 standard) to the merger, operating within Scotland and to the Shetland Islands, Western Isles, Orkney Islands, Northern Ireland and Ireland. Manx Airlines (Europe) has contributed a BAe 146-200, nine ATPs, 13 Jetstream 41s and two Jetstream 31s.

Air UK is Britain's third largest scheduled airline, with over 1,600 domestic and international flights each week. It flies to 15 destinations within the UK plus services to Belgium, the Czech Republic, Denmark, France, Germany, Holland, Italy, Norway, Spain and Switzerland. It was founded on 1 January 1980 through the merger of Air Anglia, British Island Airways, Air West and Air Wales, and currently employs some 1,600 people.

In the latest full year, Air UK carried about 3 million passengers. It has a fleet of 11 Fokker 100s, ten BAe 146-300s, one BAe 146-100, nine Fokker 50s and five F27s. The charter airline Air UK Leisure (operating three A320s, with one A321-200 for spring 1997 delivery) is to fully merge with Leisure International Airways (two 767-300ERs) in 1997. Leisure International Airways itself is the official charter airline of Unijet (which has a 40 per cent stake and Air UK 30 per cent).

Air UK
Address: Stansted Airport,
Stansted House, Essex CM24 1AE, UK.
Telephone: +44 1279 660400
Fax: +44 1279 660330

British Airways is the UK's flag airline, with a genealogy that can be traced back to 1919 through a succession of former airlines of major historical importance that include BOAC (1940 formation), Imperial Airways (1924), and the four former companies that merged into Imperial Airways (Daimler Air Hire/Daimler Airways of 1919/1921 which succeeded the inaugural AT&T; Handley-Page Transport of 1919; Instone Airline of 1920; and British Marine Air Navigation of 1923). It launched the world's first supersonic passenger service (simultaneously with Air France) in January 1976 and in February 1987 was privatized.

Today, British Airways also has a 49.9 per cent holding in TAT European Airlines (with an option to purchase the remaining shares on or before April 1997), a 25 per cent holding in Qantas, plus other significant holdings in USAir, Deutsche BA and Air Mauritius. Also, through a franchise partner arrangement, various other airlines now carry the BA livery and operate within the British Airways/British Airways Express system under the BA flight prefix (Brymon Airways, CityFlyer Express, GB Airways, British Regional Airlines, Maersk Air and Sun Air,

which together fly to 81 destinations in the UK, Ireland, continental Europe and North Africa).

British Airways itself is the world's eighth largest airline in terms of the total number of passengers carried and freight tonne-kilometres flown in a year (according to the latest available figures), standing at 30,202,000 for scheduled passengers. When extracting the figures for passengers carried on international flights only, BA becomes the world's number one airline, at 23,933,000. RPK for mainline scheduled services for the latest year stands at 87,395 million from an ASK of 122,063 million. Passenger load factor is 71.6 per cent. The number of passengers carried, when including those of Deutsche BA and TAT subsidiaries, rises to 35,643,000. Employment total then stood at 53,060 (the average for the year), including 2,926 pilots and co-pilots, but recent cuts are reducing the workforce by some 5,000.

The BA route network of mainline scheduled destinations comprises 20 in the UK, 62 in continental Europe, 21 in the USA, three in Canada, Bermuda, seven in Latin America, nine in the Caribbean, 13 in the Middle East, 13 in Africa, two in the Indian Ocean (Mauritius and Seychelles), seven in India, 12 in the Far East (including T'aipei served by British Asia Airways), and four in Australasia. The total number of countries served by scheduled flights is 83.

British Airways has a fleet of around 250 aircraft, when including aircraft operated by its wholly-owned subsidiaries and those on lease. This comprises seven Concordes, over 60 747s (thirty-two 747-400s were on order in September 1996), ten 777s (from 18 firm orders, plus options), 25 767-300s, 44 767-200s, 32 737-200s, 35 737-400s, ten A320s, seven DC-10-30s, 14 ATPs, five Dash 7s and four Dash 8s. Three 757-200s are among new aircraft ordered in September 1996.

British Airways
Address: Speedbird House, PO Box 10,
Heathrow Airport (London),
Hounslow TW6 2JA, UK.
Telephone: +44 181 759 5511
Fax: +44 181 562 9930

structural changes in 1995 and has acquired modern new aircraft and expanded its scheduled network, prompting the name change from the former GillAir. Its regional scheduled routes from Newcastle take in Aberdeen, Wick, Belfast and Manchester, while a Leeds/Bradford link to Edinburgh and Belfast City to Prestwick were added in 1995; other main operating hubs are Bournemouth and Stansted. About 17,500 passengers are carried on its scheduled routes each month.

Gill Airways currently flies two ATR 72-202, two ATR 42-300, two Shorts 360-300 and five Shorts 360-100 regional turboprop aircraft. In addition to maintaining these, the airline's engineering facility offers contract services to a number of other Shorts operators. Besides operating its own scheduled services, Gill Airways sometimes leases out aircraft, including wet-lease arrangements for the ATRs to Air UK, and flies overnight services on behalf of the Royal Mail. *Ad hoc* charters include both passenger and freight operations, particularly in support of the offshore oil and gas industries.

Gill Airways
Address: New Aviation House,
Newcastle Airport, Woolsington,
Newcastle upon Tyne NE13 8BT, UK.
Telephone: +44 191 214 6600
Fax: +44 191 214 6699

British Midland is the UK's second largest scheduled airline. It has Airlines of Britain Holding PLC as its parent company (also the parent of British Regional Airlines and Business Air). It restricts itself to airline-related business only, and in addition to its airline operations it carries out maintenance for other airlines and has its own telephone credit card and other products, but all within the airline remit.

Founded in 1938 as Derby Aviation, British Midland carried 5.6 million passengers in the latest full year (53 per cent international and 47 per cent domestic), achieving a load factor of 61.5 per cent. In 1995 it launched eight new routes, giving the airline an extensive domestic network from various hubs and international/regional links to Ireland, Northern Ireland, Spain, the Balearic Islands, France, Switzerland, Belgium, Germany, Netherlands, the Czech Republic, Denmark and Norway.

Replacement of older Stage 2 noise certified

aircraft accelerated in 1995, and by 1996 British Midland's entire fleet comprised Stage 3 types, namely 12 737-500s, six 737-400s, five 737-300s, three Fokker 70s and four Fokker 100s; the last DC-9 was taken out of service in April 1996, while its last ATP and Jetstream 41 are now operated by British Regional Airlines. British Midland has 14 code-share agreements with other international carriers, among the latest being Airlanka and Royal Brunei.

British Midland
Address: Donington Hall, Castle Donington,
Derby DE74 2SB, UK.
Telephone: +44 1332 854000
Fax: +44 1332 854662

Gill Airways is a leading independent UK scheduled and charter airline, with over 25 years of continuous service. Based in Newcastle, it underwent major

TOP
British Airways Boeing 737-400

ABOVE
British Midland Fokker 70

OPPOSITE, TOP
Boeing 777 in the livery of Emirates Airlines

OPPOSITE, BELOW
Air UK British Aerospace 146-300 for 110 passengers

East, Mahe Island and Singapore.

JEA has a history that can be traced back to Intra Airways, based in the Channel Islands, and was itself founded on 1 November 1979. Currently employing 678 staff, the airline has a fleet of seven BAe 146s, three Shorts 360s and seven F27 Series 500s. The latest figures provided showed that 1,088,000 passengers were carried over a 12-month period, giving an RPK for its scheduled services alone of 359 million, an increase over the previous year of 18 per cent.

Jersey European Airways
Address: Exeter Airport, Exeter,
Devon EX5 2BD, UK.
Telephone: +44 1392 366669
Fax: +44 1392 366151

The previously mentioned British Regional Airlines is a company of British Regional Airlines (Holdings) Limited, itself part of Airlines of Britain Holding PLC. However, Manx Airlines (not to be confused with the former Manx Airlines Europe) continues to operate under its own name, even though it is part of the same holding companies.

Founded on 1 November 1982, Manx Airlines actually has a history that goes back to Manx Air Charters of 1947, which inaugurated scheduled services in May 1950. Today, Manx Airlines operates one BAe 146-200 and four ATPs between 17 UK destinations (when including the summer seasonal points of Cork and Newcastle). It has 496 employees, of which 51 are flight deck crew. In the first five months of 1996 it carried 208,987 passengers.

Manx Airlines
Address: Isle of Man (Ronaldsway) Airport, Ballasalla,
Isle of Man IM9 2JE, UK.
Telephone: +44 1624 826000
Fax: +44 1624 826001

five A340 300s, while two 747 400s and two A340-300s will join the fleet in 1997.

Virgin now flies to New York, Washington, Los Angeles, San Francisco, Hong Kong, Japan and Athens from London's Heathrow; to Orlando, Boston and Miami from Gatwick; and Orlando from Manchester. It has code-sharing arrangements with Delta Air Lines, Malaysia Airlines and British Midland, plus a marketing alliance with Ansett Australia. In the latest full year it carried 2,107,501 passengers.

Virgin Atlantic Airways
Address: Crawley Business Quarter, Site D,
Fleming Way, Crawley, West Sussex, UK.
Telephone: +44 1293 747373
Fax: +44 1293 538337

Of the non-IATA UK airlines, which include Air 2000 (a subsidiary of First Choice Holidays with four A320s and 14 757s) plus many other large and smaller airlines, space permits coverage of just a single example. This is Britannia Airways, which undertakes international flights on behalf of its parent company, Thompson Holidays, and is stated by the company to be the world's largest charter airline.

Britannia has a fleet of three 767-304ERs, six 767-204ERs, five 757-204ERs and 14 757-204s. It also has orders and options for an additional five 767-300s, for delivery over the coming five years under its rolling programme of fleet modernization to replace existing 757 and 767-200 aircraft.

With base airports at Birmingham, Bristol, Cardiff, East Midlands, Gatwick, Glasgow, Leeds/Bradford, Luton, Manchester, Newcastle and Stansted, it flies to many destinations throughout Europe, to the Canary Islands, the Caribbean, North and Central America, Africa, the Middle East and the Indian sub-continent, Indonesia, Australia and New Zealand. In the latest full year it carried 7,959,349 passengers and accumulated an RPK of 91,430 million.

Britannia Airways
Address: Britannia House,
London Luton Airport,
Bedfordshire LU2 9ND, UK.
Telephone: +44 1582 424155
Fax: +44 1582 458594

LEFT
Virgin Atlantic Airways Boeing 747-400

OPPOSITE, ABOVE
Gill Airways ATR 72-202

OPPOSITE, BELOW
Manx Airlines BAe 146-200, still using the Isle of Man's three-legged motif

PAGES 70-71
Jersey European Airways BAe 146-200 (McIntosh)

INSET LEFT (Page 70)
Alaska Airlines tail livery, showing the familar Eskimo, behind a Horizon Air Dornier 328.

INSET RIGHT (Page 71)
America West Airlines Airbus A320, with the new paint scheme and livery

Jersey European Airways is a member of the Walker Aviation Group of companies and is said to be the largest domestic carrier and the fourth largest overall operating from London's Gatwick airport. It is the major carrier to and from the Channel Islands and Northern Ireland, while within its 14 scheduled destinations can also be counted the Isle of Man and Marseille. It also has interline agreements with 16 international carriers, offering connections to North America, Continental Europe, Africa, the Middle

Founded in 1984, and inaugurating services on 22 June with a connection between Gatwick and New York (Newark), Virgin Atlantic Airways has since become Britain's second largest longhaul airline. In 1985, Virgin Cargo and Virgin Holidays were established, and by September 1987 the then small airline's one millionth transatlantic passenger had been carried on one of its two 747-200s. Expansion has since been rapid and today it operates one 747-100, five 747-200s, three 747-400s, an A320-211 and

United States of America

The USA is home to the world's six largest airlines in terms of overall passengers carried. Domestic routes are a high priority, however, as becomes clear when it is realized that over 830 localities in the USA handle scheduled flights but only one US airline features in the world's top five airlines in terms of the number of passengers carried internationally (according to the last figures received at the time of writing).

There are over 225 airlines in the USA that fall within the terms of this book, a number that would vastly increase if smaller and air taxi operators were also to be added. Of this total, 15 are IATA members, according to the latest literature, and it is upon these that the bulk of the text applies.

Alaska Airlines can trace its history to McGee Airways, which began flights between Anchorage and Bristol Bay in 1932. Its present name was adopted in 1944, and four years later its DC-4s were used during the Berlin airlift. In 1985 the Alaska Air Group was founded as a holding company for the airline.

Use of a revolutionary 'fog busting' head-up flight guidance system in 1989 allowed Alaska to become the first airline in the world to manually land a passenger-carrying jet (727) in FAA Category III weather conditions, while in the following year the guidance system permitted an Alaska 727 to become the first passenger jet to take off in under 600 feet (183 m) of runway visibility. In 1995 it became the first US airline to book travel and sell tickets via the Internet.

With a fleet of 44 MD-80s, 22 737-400s (12 more ordered in September 1996, with 12 on option) and eight 737-200Cs, Alaska Airlines carried 10.1 million passengers over an accumulated RPK of 13.8 billion in the latest full year, achieving a passenger load factor of 61.8 per cent. It then had 7,379 employees. Its sister airline in the Alaska Airlines Group is Horizon Air, a regional carrier which serves 39 cities in the Pacific Northwest, Montana, California and Canada. Both Alaska and Horizon are marketing partners with Northwest Airlines through code sharing and reciprocal Frequent Flyer programme agreements.

Alaska Airlines itself operates to 45 domestic and international cities, of which Gustavus is the only seasonal service; Vancouver joined the network in May 1996. International routes are to Magadan, Khabarovsk, Petropavlovsk and Vladivostok in Russia and Los Cabos, Mazatlan and Puerto Vallarta in Mexico. In addition to cargo carried on regularly scheduled passenger flights, it undertakes after-hours all-cargo flights. It also offers passenger charters at weekends and in the evenings, and charters include regular flights to two military bases in the Aleutians. In addition, several smaller airlines operate a feeder service under the combined name Alaska Airlines Commuter Service.

Alaska Airlines
Address: 19300 Pacific Highway South,
Seattle, WA 98188, USA.
Telephone: +1 206 433 3200
Fax: +1 206 433 3379

Aloha Airlines is the principal subsidiary of Aloha Airgroup Inc., a Hawaii-based aviation services corporation. It began as the charter operator Trans-Pacific Airlines on 26 July 1946, becoming a certificated scheduled airline on 6 June 1949 and taking its present name in 1958. As of May 1996 it had 2,235 employees, while in July 1996 its fleet of ten 737-200s and five 737-200QCs were performing 1,375 weekly inter-island flights to Lihue (Kauai), Honolulu (Oahu), Kahului (Maui), Kona and Hilo (Hawaii).

In the latest full year, Aloha carried some 5.1 million passengers and 130.1 million pounds (59 million kg) of freight, the latter during both daytime passenger flights and at night using the QC quick-change aircraft that convert from passenger to all-cargo configuration in about 30 minutes. Its sister airline, Island Air, provides services to eight community and resort destinations on five islands using five Twin Otters and two Dash 8s.

Aloha Airlines
Address: PO Box 30028, Honolulu,
Hawaii 96820-0028, USA.
Telephone: +1 808 836 4113
Fax: +1 808 836 0303

America West Airlines is alphabetically the third US IATA airline. It is a major operator based in Phoenix, with other hubs at Las Vegas and Port Columbus (Ohio). Incorporated in September 1981, it inaugurated services on 1 August 1983 with three aircraft and 280 employees.

The current fleet of 99 aircraft comprises 61 737s, 14 757s and 24 A320s, the latter being its latest additions. In November 1996 it offered a total of 91 destinations (including 48 domestic, five in Mexico and one in Canada), when encompassing 19 code-shared via Continental Airlines and 18 code-shared with the commuter service America West Express which is operated by the Mesa Air Group (said to be the largest regional airline system in the world). The latest service to Miami was initiated on 15 November 1996. Approximately 10,000 people are employed.

America West Airlines
Address: 4000 East Sky Harbor Blvd,
Phoenix, Arizona 85034, USA.
Telephone: +1 602 693 5732
Fax: +1 602 693 5546

American Airlines, the world's second largest airline in terms of passengers carried on scheduled flights (at the time of writing), was founded in 1934 from the former American Airways, itself of 1930 creation from the amalgamation of five earlier carriers. Today, American Airlines employs some 83,900 staff as a core business of the parent company, AMR Corporation, operating within AMR's Airline Group which consists primarily of American's Passenger and Cargo divisions plus AMR Eagle.

The American Airlines Passenger Division undertakes scheduled jet services to 164 destinations, primarily in North America, the Caribbean, Latin America, Europe and the Pacific. Its Cargo Division provides a full range of freight and mail services throughout the airline's system. AMR Eagle owns the four regional airlines which operate as American

Eagle, namely Executive Airlines (36 ATRs and Shorts 360s); Flagship Airlines (82 ATR 42s, Saab 340Bs and Jetstream 32s); Simmons Airlines (90 Saab 340A/Bs and ATRs) and Wings West Airlines (57 Saab 340Bs and Jetstream 32s). The American Eagle airlines provide connecting turboprop services at seven high-traffic US cities to smaller markets throughout the USA, Canada, the Bahamas and the Caribbean.

American Airlines has hubs at Chicago O'Hare International, Dallas/Fort Worth International, Miami International and San Juan Luis Muñoz Marin International airports, and benefits from code-sharing agreements with British Midland, Canadian Airlines, Gulf Air, Qantas and South African Airways. Its huge fleet comprises 35 A300-600Rs, 41 767-300ERs, 22 767-200ERs, eight 767-200s, 86 757-200s, 81 727-200s, 75 Fokker 100s, 18 MD-11s, 17 DC-10-10s, five DC-10-30s and 260 MD-80s, making a total of 648 active airliners (more Fokker 100s and MD-11s on option).

On an average day, American Airlines will undertake more than 2,200 flights, receive more than 343,000 reservation calls, handle over 304,000 items of luggage and serve more than 196,000 meals and snacks. On one record-breaking day alone (30 June 1995) it accumulated an astonishing

377,260,000 passenger-miles (607,141,000 passenger-km).

American Airlines
Address: PO Box 619616,
Dallas/Fort Worth Airport,
Texas 75261-9616, USA.
Telephone: +1 817 963 1234
Fax: +1 817 967 4044

OPPOSITE
A non-IATA airline based on Honolulu is Hawaiian Airlines, which has a fleet of eight DC-10s (one shown) plus many DC-9-50s, DC-8s and Dash 7s for services between Oahu, Kauai, Molokai, Lanai, Maui and Hawaii, as well as to Seattle, Portland, San Francisco, Las Vegas and Los Angeles on the US mainland, and to Samoa and Tahiti

BELOW
American Airlines is the world's largest operator of Fokker 100s

Continental Airlines can trace its genealogy to Varney Air Lines, which operated Government contract mail runs from 6 April 1926. Later becoming Varney Speed Lines and Varney Air Transport, it was renamed Continental Air Lines on 1 July 1937.

At the time of writing, Continental was the world's sixth largest airline in terms of scheduled passengers carried. With hubs that include Houston, Cleveland, Denver and Newark, its domestic network of 90 points is joined by 56 international destinations in the Americas, Australia, New Zealand, Indonesia, the Pacific and Europe.

Continental also has a regional airlines division, known as Continental Express, flying from some of the hubs using turboprop airliners that include ATRs, Beech 1900Ds and Brasilias.

Continental Airlines has a fleet of over 320 US-built pure-jets (the three A300s were not in use according to Airbus Industrie listings in August 1996). With many new 737-500s, 767-300s and 777s entering service, plus more 757-200s, Boeings represent the largest element of the fleet, and in particular 737s (727s and a tiny number of 747s were also present). From McDonnell Douglas has come about 67 MD-80s, supported by remaining DC-10s and DC-9s.

Continental Airlines
Address: PO Box 4607,
77210-4607 Houston, Texas, USA.
Telephone: +1 713 834 5000
Fax: +1 713 834 4085, 2087

In terms of passengers carried on scheduled flights,

Delta Air Lines is the largest airline of all. Indeed, on 31 March 1996 the airline established a world record, when the 2-millionth passenger boarded a Delta flight at Hartsfield Atlanta International Airport, the first time this number had ever been reached at a single airport during a single month anywhere in the world. On a wider scale, the latest available full year figures showed that Delta carried a total of 89,108,028 passengers, while the airline itself, its Delta Connection carriers and its worldwide partners then operated more than 4,900 flights each day to over 300 cities in 32 countries (*see below*).

Delta's history can be traced to Delta Air Service, established in 1924 at Monroe, Louisiana, as a purely agricultural crop-dusting company. Passenger services started in 1929 with a five-passenger Travel Air 6000 aircraft flying from Dallas (Texas) to Jackson (Mississippi).

In 1996 Delta had a fleet of some 540 jet aircraft, including 120 MD-88s, 67 737s, 86 757-200s, 58 767s, 11 MD-11s and 11 MD-90s, plus many 727-200s, and TriStars. It then held orders and options for over 200 additional aircraft for delivery over the next ten years (22 737-300s, 757-200s, 767-300ERs, MD-11s and MD-90s for delivery in 1997 alone).

Employing more than 59,000 people, Delta operates over 2,500 flights each day to 197 cities in 26 countries. Its six major hubs in the US are Atlanta, Dallas/Fort Worth, Cincinnati, Salt Lake City, Los Angeles and Orlando, while the Pacific hub is at Portland (Oregon), the Atlantic hub at New York's John F. Kennedy Airport and a European hub at Frankfurt in Germany.

The Delta Connection carriers are ASA, Business Express, Comair and SkyWest,

co-ordinating their schedules with Delta Air Lines to connect an additional 94 cities.

Delta Air Lines
Address: 1020 Delta Boulevard,
30320 Atlanta, Georgia, USA.
Telephone: +1 404 715 2600
Fax: +1 404 715 5876

Federal Express Corporation, trading as FedEx, is claimed to be the world's largest express transportation company. Commencing operations on 17 April 1973, by mid-1996 it had approximately 121,000 employees worldwide.

In addition to a vast road vehicle fleet of more than 37,000 vehicles worldwide, it has the use of some 553 aircraft, comprising 17 MD-11s, 18 A300s, 22 A310s, four 747s, 35 DC-10s, 163 727s, 262 Cessna 208s and 32 F27s (more MD-11s, A300s and other types are on order). An average of 2,153,041 pounds (976,602 kg) of airfreight was carried each day in 1995.

Federal Express Corporation (FedEx)
Address: PO Box 727,
Memphis, TN 38194-1850, USA.
Telephone: +1 901 395 3460

Alphabetically after Landair International Airlines of Greeneville comes another IATA member, Northwest Airlines, the largest subsidiary of Northwest Airlines Corporation. Northwest is claimed to be the world's fourth largest airline and America's oldest carrier with continuous name identification. It began in October 1926 flying mail between Minneapolis/St Paul and Chicago, with passenger services starting in 1927. The airline pioneered the 'Great Circle' or polar route to the Orient and has operated across the Pacific Ocean longer than any other carrier. Today it employs 45,000 persons.

Northwest and its partner airlines serve more than 390 cities in 80 countries in North and South America, Europe, Asia, Africa and Australia. The Northwest and Northwest Airlink domestic network spans 48 states and the District of Columbia, covering 229 airports, while Northwest's own international network reaches 38 foreign airports. Hub cities are Detroit, Minneapolis/St Paul, Memphis and Tokyo. It strengthened its US route system by acquiring Republic Airlines in 1986 and by adopting a marketing/code-share agreement with Alaska Airlines in September 1995, while in 1993 Northwest and KLM formed a unique alliance with anti-trust immunity that offers code-sharing opportunities. It also has marketing partnerships with several regional airlines, operating Northwest Airlink (including Horizon Air – (see Page 72 Alaska Airlines).

Northwest's fleet has 388 aircraft, encompassing 47 727-200s, 41 747s, 38 757-200s, eight MD-80s, 175 DC-9s, 29 DC-10-30/-40s and 50 A320s, while 75 aircraft on order include four 747-400s, 35 757-200s, 20 A320s and 16 A330s. It is also one of the largest cargo airlines, operating eight dedicated 747-200 freighters (included in the airline's total of 388).

In the latest full year, Northwest carried 49.3 million passengers on scheduled services, an increase of 8.4 per cent over the previous 12 months. The accumulated RPK was 100,608.5 million.

Northwest Airlines
Address: 5101 Northwest Drive,
St Paul, MN 55111-3034, USA.
Telephone: +1 612 726 2331
Fax: +1 612 726 3942

IATA airline Tower Air, at JFK International Airport in New York, operates nearly 20 747s for scheduled and charter services within the USA and also to points in India, Israel, Europe, the Pacific and the Far East.

One of the all-time great airlines is Trans World Airlines (TWA), originally founded on 13 July 1925 as Western Air Express. Transcontinental Air Transport inaugurated a US coast-to-coast air/rail service in 1929, and on 1 October 1930 Transcontinental and part of Western Air Express merged to form Transcontinental and Western Air Incorporated (T&WA).

On 25 October 1930, T&WA inaugurated an all-air US coast-to-coast service taking 36 hours. International flights were inaugurated on 5 February 1946, using a Lockheed Constellation to fly the New York-Gander-Shannon-Paris route. In 1950 the corporate name was changed to Trans World Airlines. Jet services began on 20 March 1959, using a 707-

131 over the San Francisco to New York route. TWA became a public company in November 1983, while in 1995 it successfully completed a financial restructuring and introduced a new livery that October.

TWA employs 23,268 persons. TWA and TWE (Trans World Express, the airline's regional commuter service operated by Trans States Airlines) fly to over 110 destinations in the USA, the Caribbean and 12 points in Europe and the Middle East. TWA's principal hub is at St Louis but it also operates an international and domestic hub at JFK International Airport in New York, with feeder services provided by TWE (serving eight cities in the north-east and 31 in the mid-west). The latest available RPK figure for a full year of scheduled services is 40,076 million.

The TWA fleet comprises some 188 active jet aircraft, including 48 MD-80/83s, 58 DC-9s, 41 727-200s, 11 747s, 757s (see following comments), 15 767s and a reducing number of TriStars. Plans to acquire 20 new 757-200s were announced in

TOP
Northwest Airlines operates 183 MD-80s and DC-9s

ABOVE
A Boeing 747 in the new TWA livery

OPPOSITE, ABOVE
Delta Air Lines was the official airline of the 1996 Centennial Olympic Games in Atlanta (Delta Air Lines)

OPPOSITE, BELOW
FedEx Airbus A300 descends for a landing at Memphis International Airport, the world's busiest airport for cargo

February 1996, and delivery of these between July 1996 and 1999 is part of the airline's fleet modernization programme, replacing 14 TriStars. Ten A330s are also on order.

Trans World Airlines (TWA)
Address: One City Center, 515 North 6th Street,
St Louis, Missouri 63101, USA.
Telephone: +1 314 589 3000
Fax: +1 314 589 3129

United Airlines has a history dating from 1 July 1931, when United Air Lines became the holding company for the newly merged Boeing Air Transport, National Air Transport and Varney. Pacific Air Transport, often considered part of the merger, had already joined Boeing in 1928. United emerged as an operating company in 1934.

In terms of passengers carried on scheduled flights, United Airlines is today the world's third largest airline (at the time of writing). The bulk of its destinations are domestic (104), though its international network extends to 40 points in some 30 countries in the Americas, Europe, Africa, Asia, the Pacific and the Caribbean.

The United fleet of approximately 560 jet aircraft included 34 A320s and 24 747-400s in September 1996. A further 16 A320s and 24 A319s are on order as part of its modernization programme. The remainder of the fleet comprises 777s (36), 767-300ERs, 767-200s, 757s (92), 737s, 727s and DC-10s, while 19 747-400s (plus four previously ordered), six 757s and two 777s were ordered in August 1996. Options for the future include the probable huge investment in over 200 more aircraft, by far the largest proportion being 737s. United Express is the United Airlines' regional commuter service operated by several airlines.

United Airlines
Address: PO Box 66100, Elk Grove Township,
Illinois 60666, USA.
Telephone: +1 847 700 4000
Fax: +1 847 700 7345

Another giant package delivery organization is United Parcel Service of America. Its air branch, UPS Airlines, began operations in 1988 and flies nearly 200 large jet freighters (767s, 757s, 747s, 727s and DC-8s). UPS received its tenth 767 Freighter on 10 October 1996, having been the launch customer for the all-cargo 767 a year earlier.

USAir is among the world's largest airlines and has formed a major alliance with British Airways, which has a 24 per cent stake in the American carrier. It is a part of the USAir Group. It began operations in 1939 as All American Aviation, initially to deliver and collect mail from awkwardly located towns in the Allegheny Mountain area of north-eastern USA, by dropping mail containers and air-snatching suspended outward-going mail without landing.

Passenger services were inaugurated on six feeder routes in 1949, and in 1953 All American was renamed Allegheny Airlines. Through expansion and mergers, Allegheny's route network took in more of the USA, and the airline's present name was adopted in 1979 to reflect this.

Throughout expansion, USAir has maintained services with smaller towns and cities, using them as feeder points to its principal hubs. Consequently, in 1967 Allegheny Commuter was founded, now part of the USAir Express organization, which co-ordinates the flights by many smaller commuter airlines.

USAir and USAir Express serve 194 domestic destinations in North America, plus five in Canada, Bermuda, Mexico City in Latin America, ten in the Caribbean and some six in Europe, operating from four major hubs at Charlotte, Pittsburgh, Philadelphia and Baltimore/Washington. The separate USAir Shuttle operates 727s on scheduled domestic services between Washington DC, New York/La Guardia and Boston.

USAir has 12 767-200s, 40 757-200s, 54 737-400s, about 90 737-300s, 64 737-200s, 31 MD-80s, 62 DC-9-30s, 40 Fokker 100s and five F28s, while eight more 757-200s and 40 737-300s will eventually join the fleet. Allegheny Commuter, Piedmont Airlines and PSA Airlines are among USAir Express airlines and are owned by the USAir Group, adding 109 turboprop airliners (Dash 7s, Dash 8s, Jetstream 31s and Dornier 328s).

USAir
Address: 2345 Crystal Park Drive, Arlington,
Virginia 22227, USA.
Telephone: +1 800 428 4322
Fax: +1 703 418 5131

Uruguay

Uruguay has a single airport for scheduled flights at the captial Montevideo. The national airline is PLUNA (Primeras Líneas Uruguayas de Navegación Aérea), which was founded in September 1935 and inaugurated services using two de Havilland Dragonflies on 15 November 1936. It proved so successful that, a year later, a ten-passenger or freight-carrying four-engined DH.86B Express Air Liner was purchased with a Government subsidy. Presently operating three 737-200s, a DC-10-30 and a 707, it is mainly concerned with scheduled and charter regional services, though Madrid is an international destination.

Uzbekistan

This republic has two airports for scheduled flights. The national airline is Uzbekistan Airways operating out of Tashkent and Samarkand, and receiving technical assistance from Lufthansa. It has a large fleet of more than 100 aircraft for its domestic and international network (including India, Israel,

Malaysia, Turkey and the UK) of scheduled and charter services, headed by two A310s, ten Il-86s, three Tu-154Ms, a 757 and Il-114s among other types, being joined by two 767-300ERs ordered in October 1995.

Vanuatu

Vanuatu comprises 83 islands covering a distance of over 600 miles (1,000 km) in the south-west Pacific. Consequently it has 29 airports handling scheduled flights. The Government owns two airlines, of which the smaller is Vanair (Vanuatu Internal Air Services), the inter-island domestic airline with flights to all 29 destinations but particularly to the islands of Tanna, Pentecost and Espiritu Santo, using a fleet of two Islanders and four Twin Otters.

The international airline is Air Vanuatu, with connections to Auckland, Brisbane, Melbourne, Sydney, Nouméa (New Caledonia) and Nadi (Fiji). It operates one 737-400 and a Bandeirante.

Air Vanuatu (Operations) Limited
Address: 2nd Floor, Lolam House,
Kumul Highway, Port Vila, Efate Island, Vanuatu.
Telephone: +678 23 838
Fax: +678 23 250

ABOVE
Among the newest aircraft in the United Parcel Service fleet is the Boeing 767-300ER

OPPOSITE
United Airlines Airbus A320

Venezuela

Of ten or more airlines in Venezuela, two are members of IATA, namely Aérovias Venezolanas (Avensa) and Venezolana Internacional de Aviación (Viasa). Avensa, based in Caracas, is principally a domestic airline operating to 17 of the country's 24 airports handling scheduled services. It has a fleet of 15 727s, three 737s, two 757s, five DC-9s and two Convair 580s. However, it is not exclusively domestic and extends across borders into Panama City and Mexico City. It was founded on 13 May 1943, with assistance from Pan American which originally held a 23 per cent stake, and services began in May 1944 using Ford Trimotors and other aircraft. It is now Government owned.

In 1961, KLM of the Netherlands, Avensa and Línea Aeropostal Venezolana (LAV) joined forces to create Viasa as an international airline, taking over Avensa's and LAV's foreign services and with KLM performing as European agent and operating a DC-8 service for the new carrier. More than three decades later, Viasa continues this mission, though with the Government and Iberia (45 per cent) holding shares. Operating out of Caracas and Porlamar, with a fleet of seven 727s and five DC-10s, it flies scheduled services to 17 domestic and regional destinations in the Americas, ten into Europe plus winter charters to Canada.

Venezolana Internacional de Aviación (Viasa)
Address: Apartado de Correos 6857,
Caracas DF, Venezuela.
Telephone: +58 2 576 0411
Fax: +58 2 571 3731

Vietnam

Vietnam has 12 airports handling scheduled flights. Neither of its two noteworthy airlines is an IATA member, though Vietnam Airlines is the Government-owned national airline. With hubs in the capital Hanoi and the municipality Ho Chi Minh City, it has an extensive domestic network plus services to 16 international destinations which include Hong Kong and Singapore.

Not altogether surprisingly, its fleet is a mixture of older Russian aircraft and leased modern western types, with Tu-134s, Yak-40s and an Il-18 joined by eight A320s (mostly received in July-August 1996; the leasing agreement with Aerostar reportedly providing the option to purchase), three 767-300ERs, four other 767s and four ATR 72s. Two more A320s were expected in January 1997, while two Fokker

70s were required as Tu-134 replacements.

Pacific Airlines, headquartered in Ho Chi Minh City, operates domestic and international (to France, Hong Kong, India, Taiwan and Thailand) charter freight services with a 737-200 in co-operation with the French operator AOM.

Western Samoa

The islands of Savai'i and Upolu in the Pacific Ocean are connected by the domestic operations of the national airline, Polynesian Airlines (IATA member). Founded in 1959, it had been created to undertake regional flights to Apia and Pago Pago, which are now joined by other scheduled regional/international services to Australia, the Cook Islands, Fiji, New Zealand, Niue island and Tonga. The Polynesian fleet comprises two 767-200ERs, two 737s, a Twin Otter and an Islander.

Yemen

This republic has 11 airports for scheduled flights. Both of its main airlines are IATA members. The Government-owned Alyemen Airlines of Yemen, founded in 1971, has a fleet of some eight aircraft for scheduled domestic, regional and international services, including two 737-200s. It operates out of Aden.

The larger airline is Yemenia – Yemen Airways, which flies from the capital San'a'. Its roots can be traced to Yemen Airlines, which had flown fairly irregular services from 1957 with some assistance from Soviet and Yugoslav personnel, and which was reorganized in 1961 and again in 1972. The presently named airline dates from 1978. Though it is majority owned by the Government, Saudi Arabia holds a large interest.

Yemenia has an all-western fleet of some nine aircraft, comprising a 737-200, 727-200s, Twin Otters and Dash 7s. According to Airbus Industrie listings of 31 August 1996, it has two A310s on order but none in operation, these expected to be delivered in early 1997. Apart from flights to eight domestic points, it has a regional/international network to well over 20 destinations in Africa, the Middle East, Asia and Europe.

Yugoslavia

This federal republic encompasses the republics of Montenegro and Serbia plus two autonomous provinces, though the latter are administratively part of Serbia. The capital of Serbia and of the federal republic as a whole is Belgrade, which is the main base of the flag airline, Jugoslovenski Aerotransport

(JAT) or simply Yugoslav Airlines.

Yugoslav Airlines has two 737-300s, two 727-200s, seven DC-9s, a DC-10 and two ATR 72s. At the time of writing its main operations were domestic.

Zaire

This African republic has 12 airports handling scheduled services. Since Air Zaire ceased operating, it has been served principally by nine fairly small airlines, of which most offer charter services. Among those with scheduled as well as charter operations are Scibe Airlift of Zaire flying from the capital Kinshasa using a small fleet that includes two 727-100s and a 707-320C, and Shabair operating from Lubumbashi in the Shaba region with some ten jet airliners and smaller propeller types that include three 727s, a DC-10 and two BAC One-Elevens.

Zaire Express was founded in 1994. It flies out of Kinshasa and has an alliance with Sabena. Offering scheduled services over a domestic and regional network of about 14 destinations, it has three BAC One-Elevens and four or more 737-200, 727-200 and 707C types for passengers or cargo.

Zambia

Zambia has eight airports handling scheduled flights. Its newest airline is Aero Zambia, which was founded on 21 May 1994 after the cessation of Zambia Airways' operations. Aero Zambia inaugurated passenger and cargo services in March 1995 using a 737-200 and a 737-200C, both leased. It has established extensive co-operative arrangements with major airlines from some 15 countries and is expanding its domestic, regional and European route networks, taking in leased aircraft for the latter.

Zimbabwe

Zimbabwe has five airports handling scheduled flights. Both Affretair, which operates cargo flights with three DC-8Fs, and Air Zimbabwe use the capital Harare as their base. Both are Government owned and both are members of IATA. In addition to African regional destinations, Affretair flies to Egypt, the Netherlands and the UK.

Air Zimbabwe has a genealogy that can be traced to 1961 and the creation of an airline under the auspices of the Rhodesian Ministry of Transport. In the final year of its existence as Air Rhodesia (1978), one of its Viscounts carrying 56 passengers was shot down by a surface-to-air missile. Becoming Air Zimbabwe Rhodesia and then in 1980 simply Air Zimbabwe, it is the national airline with domestic flights between all five main airports, regional services to 12 African cross-border destinations, and international routes to Australia (Perth and Sydney using Qantas 747s), Cyprus, Germany and the UK. In addition to a single BAe 146 and two Fokker 50s, its fleet encompasses six Boeings as equal numbers of 767-200ERs, 737-200s and 707-320Bs.

Air Zimbabwe Corporation
Address: PO Box AP1, Harare, Zimbabwe.
Telephone: +263 4 575 111
Fax: +263 4 575 068

ABOVE
Impression of a Fokker 70 in Vietnam Airlines livery

INDEX

Page numbers in *italics* refer to illustrations